Outside the Wall

OUTSIDE
the
WALL

A PUERTO RICAN WOMAN'S STRUGGLE

Felix M. Padilla
and
Lourdes Santiago

Rutgers University Press · New Brunswick, New Jersey

Library of Congress Cataloging-in-Publication Data

Padilla, Felix M.
    Outside the wall : a Puerto Rican woman's struggle / Felix M.
Padilla and Lourdes Santiago.
        p.   cm.
    Includes index.
    ISBN 0-8135-1986-1 (cloth) — ISBN 0-8135-1987-X (pbk.)
    1. Santiago, Lourdes, 1961–   2. Prisoners' wives—United
States—Biography. 3. Puerto Ricans—United States—Biography.
I. Santiago, Lourdes, 1960–   II. Title.
HV8886.U5P34 1993
362.8'3—dc20   92-41731
                                                    CIP

British Cataloging-in-Publication information available

B
Padilla
P

Contents

Preface

This is the story of Lourdes Santiago, a woman who has struggled to maintain self-respect and dignity in spite of the social stigmatization attached to those like herself. Lourdes is a prisoner's wife. Ten years ago she decided to remain in a marriage in which she is forced to live apart from her husband. He, a known gang leader, was given a seventy-year prison term for the fatal shooting of a member of an opposing gang—a crime, Lourdes insists, he did not commit. In the process of trying to sustain her marriage Lourdes has faced numerous crises, and each time she has responded with resiliency and, ultimately, renewed faith. Although she admits to having made some mistakes along the way, she has steadily converted them into opportunities for self-improvement and empowerment.

Lourdes is an extraordinary woman, and her story is equally remarkable. She remains hopeful when success seems far out of reach; she is considerate when she could easily act enraged; and she manages to think a problem through when conditions appear most turbulent. She is a strong and noble woman whose story deserves to be told.

Although Lourdes is the co-author of this book, her job was the more demanding one, for it required her to reconsider and articulate her most painful experiences. I am indebted to Lourdes for being courageous and sharing these experiences.

I want to express my most sincere words of gratitude to my friend and colleague Teresa Cordova, now at the University of New Mexico, for reading and offering suggestions for improving the story. Teresa is a true *hermana*.

Special thanks go to Rebecca Steffes for transcribing many of the interviews I conducted with Lourdes. She also read the entire book manuscript and provided me with plenty of contextual and grammatical suggestions. *Muchas gracias, compañera!*

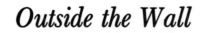

Outside the Wall

Introduction

If someone had looked into a crystal ball and said to me that this was going to happen to me, I never would have believed it. I grew up in the Pentecostal church. I would go to church, to the services. I was involved with the youth, going on camping trips. I grew up separated from the neighborhood kids that people believed were doing bad things. I was perceived so differently from my friends because I was going to church. I wanted everything so perfect.

I remember growing up and watching the Miss America pageant, and when Miss Puerto Rico won the crown my father was so proud—that's what he wanted us to do. He wanted us to lead a successful life. So, there was no way I was going to lose when I was coming up through this kind of upbringing.

And what happens? Well, my husband and I have been married for fourteen years; we were married at an early age—he was eighteen, and I was fifteen—and for the majority of this time our relationship as husband and wife has been carried out with him inside prison walls and me on the outside. My husband was a gang leader, who was charged with committing a major crime. His sentence is seventy years.

He's been in prison for nine years. By statistics married life is very difficult to maintain. It is hard enough for two people under the same roof living together to keep their marriage—imagine when they are separated, in two different places. That's how things have been for the last nine years—he's inside, and I'm out here. But we are making it work. We are not giving up.

These were the first reflections about her life which Lourdes shared with me. The day was Monday, 29 October 1990, and I had just completed the first of many interviews I would conduct with Lourdes over the next two years.

I first met Lourdes in early June 1990 during a visit I was making to one of the maximum-security prisons in the state of Illinois. I was there with my friend Hector to meet and speak for the first time with one of his friends, who was an inmate. Hector was helping me gather information on the history of a Puerto Rican youth gang in Chicago, the Diamonds, for a book I was writing at the time (Padilla 1992). Hector was confident that his friend could help me, so he invited me along on his next visit to the prison.

That day Lourdes was also at the penitentiary on a visit. Her visit, however, was part of a weekly ritual she had carried out since 1981, when her husband was given a seventy-year sentence for the fatal shooting of a member of an opposing gang. Every Saturday she went to see her husband. During the time that we spent meeting and talking about her life history—and before the summer of 1991, when her husband was transferred to a New Jersey prison—only on several occasions was Lourdes not able to make her Saturday visits. I recall one time she came down with a bad cold; another time her car broke down. Almost nothing prevented Lourdes from visiting her husband once a week.

My initial encounter with Lourdes took place in the waiting room of the prison. We were introduced by Hector, who is also a friend of Lourdes. We simply exchanged casual hellos. Lourdes did not appear to have the time to say any more than that, for she was busy talking to other Latino visitors. She moved about the waiting room, going to different people and engaging in conversation. I would discover later that Lourdes knew many of these visitors, and she was constantly reminding and encouraging them to continue their ongoing contact with the inmates they were there to see.

Two weeks after this brief meeting Lourdes asked Hector to invite me to attend a meeting for individuals who were working on developing an organization whose aim was to deal with issues facing family members of inmates who were serving time in the state's prison system. I called Lourdes and told her that I was flattered over the invitation but assured her that I knew little about such issues. She was not about to take no for an answer. She said that I could still help—particularly, in working with prospective members on the more technical elements of developing and maintaining a formal organization. She thought that, since I was a sociology professor, I would know something about the technicalities and procedures involved in building an organization.

I decided to participate and get involved in what the group was trying to do. When the organization became an official and chartered entity under the name of Citizens Working for Prison Reform, I was made one of its board members. For the most part the organization served as a support group, helping mostly women to cope with the incarceration of their son, husband, boyfriend, or brother.

Since my first meeting with Lourdes in June 1990, I have participated in organizational meetings once a month and other social and cultural activities, some related to the prison reform group, others not. People who attended the organizational meetings and social activities were relatives or friends of inmates. Most of the board members and those who participated in the meetings and other activities were women. There were some male members within the organization who were friends of inmates or who represented social service agencies handling juvenile delinquency (in cases in which a juvenile was in prison). It was the women, however, who shouldered most of the responsibility for carrying out the fundamental functions of the organization.

Although my involvement with the organization was meant to help with its development, by attending and participating in various meetings and group activities, I was able to learn precious details about the concerns and problems central to the lives of those around me.

In particular, I learned some of what makes Lourdes's life distinctive. As a leader, Lourdes was given the task of moderating group discussions. When speaking to the group, she always used her personal story to inspire those present to verbalize their own stories, their own individual and family distress. Lourdes believed that, by sharing her experiences, others would recognize that they were not alone, that others are living with similar circumstances. If the purpose of the organization was to look for ways that could best remedy their collective conditions, this was possible, Lourdes reasoned, only after the women gained the confidence to begin opening up and telling their stories in public. As Lourdes stated in one of the early meetings I attended:

I used to be to myself. I didn't want people to know what had happened to me. And when I finally decided to accept my condition, to accept the fact that my husband is an inmate, the more mothers, wives, and sisters I discovered out there who wanted to speak out. But they, like me, are afraid. It's just that we sometimes think that this is only happening to me *and no one else. I would tell these women to come and join us, because here we are going to make others feel better, and we're going to fight together so our husbands will not have to suffer the way they do. If we remain quiet, we're not going to be of any help to them. We must do it together, just like everything else we've done in our lives.*

Listening to Lourdes during these early meetings made it clear that she was courageous. It was astonishing to witness Lourdes disclose in public very personal and stressful facts about her life. Not many of us are willing to submit to this kind of self-disclosure, but to Lourdes it is the only way to touch and motivate others.

My participation in meetings and activities of the organization enabled me to observe how Lourdes's deep caring for other women and families translated into action. It was common to hear Lourdes talk about having picked up and driven several women to the prison on her Saturday visits, before her husband was transferred to another state. She has also mentioned that she has at times translated (from English into Spanish) documents and forms sent by prison officials to the families of inmates. And how often is she called upon by other women to explain technical points regarding conditions or events at the prison which their son, husband, boyfriend, or brother was facing. On occasion Lourdes is called to investigate a case in which prison officials have moved an inmate to another prison without notifying the family.

It was remarkable to me that Lourdes could put out such effort while working in a very demanding and time-consuming job, keeping a heavy religious schedule, and working to sustain her marriage.

Lourdes works full time in a community-based organization as supervisor of a team of individuals who provide home care to handicapped and disabled individuals and the elderly. In this line of work Lourdes spends a great deal of time responding to her clients' needs. Her job is truly service oriented.

Lourdes's involvement in the Pentecostal church includes attending services four times a week, in addition to teaching Sunday school. She often travels to other cities and states for conferences and meetings as a representative of her church. Many of these trips keep her away from her home for days.

And, although her husband is serving a prison term that could very well keep the two separated for many years, Lourdes is emotionally and physically committed to preserving their marriage. Although she can no longer visit her husband every Saturday—because he is in another state—she talks to him on the phone several times a week. She often writes to him at least a letter a week. She also maintains her home to make it look ready for him, as if he were arriving at any time—she is forever expecting his arrival. I recall visiting her house for the first time and thinking that, indeed, a married couple lived there. Pictures of their wedding, her husband, and their families decorate the house. And so did the many certificates, diplomas, and other recognition awards as well as toys and stuffed animals.

Maintaining a marital relationship with her husband and working with family members of other inmates to protect and enhance the human rights of prisoners—individuals who society defines and treats as worthless and then condemns to a life of humiliation as social outcasts—represent for Lourdes forms of resistance. Rather than becoming desperate and cynical, Lourdes has decided to use her conditions of suffering as the foundation for better understanding, critiquing, and opposing an unsympathetic society. In other words, her status as a prisoner's wife has inspired her to maintain her dignity and to deepen her commitment to resisting injustice.

The resistance Lourdes has cultivated to counter societal afflictions has also been ignited by a love that leads her to value herself and other people and to hope for more than the dominant society has been willing to grant to individuals like her. As theologian Sharon Welch puts it: "acts of love [are] affirmations of the delightfulness and profundity of life. Such acts declare the tragedy of what is lost because of injustice, and they celebrate the satisfaction of life lived under conditions of justice. A deep joy accompanies the cycle of providing shelter and food, nurturing the young, and celebrating the beauty of life in art, music and poetry" (1990, 165).

Overall, Lourdes's acts of resistance are informed by a cultural perspective that precludes self-pity; it is a perspective that provides for understanding both suffering and the need for and meaning of compassion. Lourdes's cultural perspective teaches that life and suffering themselves are teachers, that even loneliness has a purpose, and that sadness can positively be the wellspring of creativity. Her perspective stems from the understanding that oppressed and suffering people cannot now, or ever, take a rest from opposing systems of injustice which plague them, for they are its target.

What has made Lourdes the way she is? What events and experiences illuminated her development to make her the person she is? How did she feel about the individuals and societal conditions that shaped her life, and how did she respond to them? These were some of my initial questions about Lourdes's life. The more I learned of her life experiences and the views and feelings she holds toward herself and other people and toward specific social issues and problems, the more I thought it would be a good idea to document her story.

After attending several organizational meetings and speaking with Lourdes at her work and over lunch about issues concerning the organization she was trying to develop, I mentioned the idea of my interviewing her over a period of time for the purpose of writing her story. To my surprise she readily agreed. It seemed as if she had been waiting to be asked to engage in this, another, project. Although she was aware that, in recounting her past, she would have to bring up some painful memories, yet she felt she had almost an obligation to do so:

I have thought about doing the story myself. I have spoken to my husband about it, and he said to go with it, but the problem is time. I just don't have any. Also, I sat once and wrote a few pages; when I read them I cried and cried. I just couldn't go on. I couldn't believe how much I had gone through. But now I think it can be done, if I just tell it to you, and you write it. There's no question that I want to do this project. I owe it to other women, other wives, other mothers, and other families. So, hopefully, some people will read it and not suffer like I have. If that happens, then that is my contribution.

She added, however: "I would not know where to begin, because there's so much to tell. Ask me some questions so I'll know what you're interested about. To me this would be the easiest way to tell what my story is about." "That is exactly how we will do it," I told her, then: "I am not completely certain about any particular areas I want to emphasize at this point. Instead, I will look to you to describe those events you believe are most significant in your life and what they have meant to you. At a later time I might need to ask you additional questions to help fill out places in the story. But, throughout, everything will be open for you to comment on any aspect of your life."

Undoubtedly, Lourdes possesses sufficient self-esteem and strong feelings of self-worth to allow me to record her story and later sharing it. Several years ago Lourdes would not have accepted going public with her story.

Also, I believe that Lourdes confided in me because I was someone that one of her friends endorsed. In addition, she had read a draft of my 1992 book, *The Gang as an American Enterprise*, which I was finishing about the time I met her, and she expressed an appreciation for the way I had presented and analyzed the Diamonds' story. She envisioned her life story receiving the same kind of treatment.

My willingness to participate in the organization that Lourdes was creating was another reason she decided to reveal her life experiences to me. Through the various organization meetings and social and cultural activities it sponsored, we were able to develop a relationship as friends. She understood that my involvement in the organization and my commitment to help as much as I could were symbolic of our friendship. As such, this work was predicated on mutual trust and esteem.

Nearly three months after our initial meeting and continuing for a period of nearly twenty-four months, we would meet at her office or mine during the day, but mostly at her house after working hours, and we would tape-record interview after interview. The routine became fairly standard: I would stop at a restaurant, usually Puerto Rican or Chinese, and buy food to bring to our meetings. Shortly after arriving at Lourdes's house, we would eat, for about an hour; often we were joined by her brother. During our dinner conversations we usually talked about happenings that had little to do with the subjects and themes we would discuss in the interview session. When the meal was over Lourdes's brother would leave, and we would begin the formal interviewing.

Being tape-recorded did not discourage Lourdes from telling her story as completely as possible. She was mainly concerned with not revealing the names of individuals and places, fearing that these individuals could be additionally tormented if their identities were uncovered. I promised that I would leave out all the names in transcribing the interviews. In the text of the book the few names that appear are fictitious, with the exception of Lourdes's. One day I spoke to her about making up a name that would protect her own identity, and in a very serious way she replied, "I've been thinking about this issue for some time now, and I've decided to keep my real name in the book." I was somewhat surprised by her response; after all, the book is bound to make her story widely known. I imagined that Lourdes would not want some of her friends and acquaintances to learn about this side of her life. She saw it differently:

My feeling is that, without my name, the book doesn't appear real. I want people to be able to say, "Yes, this is a true story because it happened to this woman, and her name is Lourdes." And there will be people out there who know me or heard of me and can confirm that all the things that we are going to present in the book in fact happened. If I'm going to reveal my story, then I want people to know that it's my story and not someone else's, a person they will not be able to recognize.

Lourdes's crowded schedule, which included individual, family, job, and church responsibilities, served to limit the amount of time that she could devote to this project at any one meeting. Lourdes agreed to do a handful of interviews a month, and, indeed, we ended up meeting and conducting two to three monthly interviews. This arrangement was agreeable with my own schedule, and it gave me time to transcribe and critically review the interviews, creating new questions to ask Lourdes during subsequent meetings on anything I found to be incomplete or unclear. A total of twenty-two interviews were conducted, producing more than five hundred and fifty single-spaced pages.

Our interview sessions lasted between two and four hours. Most of the time at the end Lourdes felt particularly exhausted from the arduous ordeal of giving detailed accounts of various painful experiences in her life. As expected, on many occasions Lourdes was on the verge of breaking down and crying, but each time she reminded herself: "I must be strong. I can't cry anymore. I have done too much of that already." I always told her that it was perfectly normal to cry again and not to feel embarrassed. This was the only viable suggestion I could offer, for I, too, was experiencing some of her grief. Lourdes would often turn the sorrow into humor by laughing away some hurtful memory. It took me a while to really understand that many times, when Lourdes would burst into spontaneous, loud laughter, she was actually preventing herself from weeping. I suggested that we could stop the interview at any time, but we always continued.

To capture Lourdes's story I employed a "life history" approach, one that emphasizes four central criteria. According to Michael McCall and Judith Wittner,

> *It pay[s] tribute to human subjectivity and creativity—showing how individuals respond to social constraints and actively assemble social worlds; it deal[s] with concrete human experiences—talk, feelings, action—through their social, and especially economic, organization (and not just their inner, psychic or biological structuring); it show[s] a naturalistic "intimate familiarity" with such experiences—abstractions untempered by close involvement are ruled out; and there [is] a self-awareness by the sociologist of the ultimate moral and political role in moving towards a social structure in which there is less exploitation, oppression, and injustice and more creativity, diversity, and equality. (1990, 52)*

Through the life history approach, then, Lourdes was able to speak directly about the ways she perceives, organizes, gives meaning to, and expresses her understanding of herself, her experiences, and her world. The life history approach makes it possible for Lourdes to voice the ways in which her understanding of the world is related to her social, cultural, and personal circumstances.

The outcome of this life history project is Lourdes's self-reported biography—her self-conscious testimony of what she wants to tell about herself as a Puerto Rican, working-class woman. Specifically, Lourdes's story provides evidence of the struggles on the part of a generation of U.S.-born and/or -raised Puerto Rican women and men against the consequences of abandonment, neglect, and exploitation of Puerto Rican people in the United States. Forced to live on the margins of society, large numbers of Puerto Ricans are barely surviving. And not possessing the fundamental resources needed to get ahead has forced some into illegal enterprising. One such activity is the youth gang and its drug-dealing operations. Lourdes's story unfolds within the context of a harsh and repressive social environment that has prompted many Puerto Rican young women and men to seek refuge in the youth gang and its complex system of drug distribution and dealing.

Just as important, the story told by Lourdes serves as evidence of the major historic role played by Puerto Rican women as creative agents of social change in their communities. Her testimony directly challenges inaccurate stereotypes about Puerto Rican and other women as submissive and subordinate counterparts to their male partners. For sure, Lourdes's and other women's lives have been shaped in part by the surrounding world (including the actions of men), but women have emphatically shaped their own lives as well as those of others.

Blanca Vasquez Erazo, a researcher at the Center for Puerto Rican Studies at Hunter College in New York, makes the following observations concerning women who have participated in the program's oral history projects: "In examining the stories Puerto Rican women were telling us, converging images began to emerge in the self-projections of the women. These powerful projections of self offer an alternative view of working-class women, conveying a sense of women as strong, resourceful, ingenious, and determined to overcome the obstacles they face daily in the world of work" (1988, 20).

Lourdes's story does not emerge simply from a context of personal achievement; instead, she offers a model for community betterment and solidarity. Her experiences point in the direction of change, possibilities not only for herself but for an entire community. Lourdes's work for justice represents a process through which the self is enlarged to include a wider community; Lourdes knows too well that she cannot be the sole bearer of change. In *A Feminist Ethic of Risk* Sharon Welch speaks to this need to work together: "The extent to which an action is an appropriate response to the needs of others is constituted as much by the possibilities it creates as by its immediate results. Responsible action does not mean one individual resolving the problems of others. It is, rather, participation in a communal work, laying the groundwork for the creative response of people in the present and in the future" (1990, 75).

The views, attitudes, and actions embodied in Lourdes's life history represent a special type of feminism, one that is rooted in a universalist and integrationist perspective, in a sense of connection and relatedness to others. When Lourdes speaks about self-liberation and feminism, labels she doesn't really like to claim for her own life, one can discern her serious commitment to the survival, maintenance, and growth of an entire community of people—male, female, the elderly, children. For her, self-liberation is synonymous with the liberation of her community and people. To be a liberated woman is necessary if Puerto Ricans are to be emancipated from the conditions of inequality and oppression to which they have been relegated by external forces. Labor historian Altagracia Ortiz has described the "work" performed by Puerto Rican women in New York City as having this same community emphasis:

> *Work among puertorriquenas* is not only what some of our women *do* in factories, stores, hospitals, schools, or offices— work activities for which they receive remuneration in the form of a "pay" that often means just meager wages that hardly support them or their families. Work for *puertorriquenas* also has come to mean those kinds of constructive *doings* that have resulted in holding their families together, in building or reconstructing their communities, . . . in continuing their struggle to survive as a people with dignity. (1992, 1–2)

Lourdes's feminism has its theological correlate, a Pentecostal theology of divine "wholesomeness," encompassing all people, both men and women, in all conditions of life (for example, race, ethnicity, and class). Her religion provides a basis for affirming the solidarity of the whole human community; in particular, it seeks to affirm women so that they are acknowledged as full partners with men, sharing in the image of God. In this way Lourdes's religious views resonate with those of some feminist scholars who, as Letty Russel describes, are "searching today for a feminist interpretation of the Bible that is rooted in the feminist critical consciousness that women and men are fully human and fully equal. This consciousness is opposed to teachings and actions that reinforce the social system that oppresses women and other groups in society" (1985, 15).

Arranging the vast information Lourdes revealed to me into her life story was a major task. Like Sidney Mintz, whose life history of a Puerto Rican sugarcane worker served as a model, I decided to organize it "on a grid, one axis being topical and the other chronological" (1974, 7). This meant developing an order of formal categories, or themes, then dividing this material according to the sequence of events in time. Family, neighborhood, and school experiences; husband-wife relations; coping (with life during the first few years of husband's incarceration); and adaptation became the leading categories I extrapolated from the accounts Lourdes gave of her life experiences. At no point did I try imposing my own conceptual categories into the story; I did not come into the project with a list of ideas which I aimed to formulate and test. Rather, I listened and let Lourdes's own account provide the information with which to frame the story.

The story's topical and chronological arrangement began to take shape after the fourth interview. By then Lourdes had provided me with about seventy-five pages of general information, with much overlap. I met with Lourdes to let her see the outline of her story which I had developed. I wanted to be certain that it was in accordance with the story's actual development. She approved of it, though there was a certain amount of information that was out of place or simply missing. After this point the interviews were geared to soliciting specific information about the events that were central to Lourdes's story.

And, from here on, every time I completed a draft of a chapter of the book I would ask Lourdes to review and critique it. When the book was finally completed she read it entirely. I tried to limit my intervention in the presentation of the text. Since the actual transcription of the interviews produced a raw and fragmented text, I made certain basic editorial and grammatical corrections to make it more readable, but these were slight. Again I shared the new version with Lourdes and asked her to examine it and to provide her own comments and suggestions.

Having Lourdes read and critique drafts of the text of her story was significant. Not only did it allow gaps to be filled and necessary corrections to be made, but just as important, it permitted Lourdes to add new and emerging meanings to her experience. The act of storytelling of this sort, in other words, has the potential for enhancing the reflexive consciousness in the narrator. As pointed out by Lawrence Watson and Maria Watson-Franks:

> We must recognize, however, that during the time he is committing his life to record, a person may experience some change of outlook or character that makes him start reassessing his life in a way that was impossible when he started. Sometimes the very act of recalling one's life can bring unexpected insights that change the view of past experiences, particularly under the promptings of the one who does the eliciting. (1985, 2–3)

Listen to Lourdes's reaction after having read chapter 1, the first piece of writing I shared with her and asked her to examine:

Felix:	Walk me through some of the things you commented on after having read the chapter.
Lourdes:	After reading it I couldn't believe that it was me who was speaking in those pages. I read it all. I couldn't stop reading it. My reaction was: "I don't like this. My story is so sad and painful. It sounds mean in some places because it provides a portrayal of people who I love as being so hard."
Felix:	What was hard about the information?
Lourdes:	My childhood years. I described how everything came about and how I grew up—and all of it got me to think again: "was it really like this? Was it different?" If I said that's the way it was, then that was how things really happened. I was holding all of it inside. I just couldn't believe it when I read it.
Felix:	Overall, what did you learn about yourself from the chapter?
Lourdes:	That I've had some rough times. It was interesting. And I know that there were some hard times, and, despite it all, I learned to take it in stride. I learned that I've come a long way. I think, more importantly, what has happened is that the interviews got me to talk and open up. I never did that before. I was always reserved.

In addition, Lourdes's reading of and reaction to the different chapters served as the confirmation she needed to continue her efforts to make changes and to fight for justice and equality. After examining the first draft of chapter 4 Lourdes said: "Sometimes we read about the years that people spend involved in some issues. We learn how they lose hope and give up. This chapter reminds me that, in spite of what I've done and gone through, that much work is ahead of us. We can't stop. I think that's the lesson that comes out of these pages."

From the very first time we started working on Lourdes's story we made the decision to present it as she was verbalizing it to me: in her words. To accomplish this, each interview was transcribed verbatim. Then, when it was transferred to the text of the story, I made only slight grammatical changes. At no time did I alter Lourdes's meaning. Of course, Lourdes would not have allowed substitutions. In addition, while reading drafts of the chapters, Lourdes occasionally changed words and restructured sentences.

So, the grammar used in Lourdes's story is correct, perhaps making some readers wonder how a person can speak so properly as if writing instead. Again, the presentation was polished so that it would read clearly. Because we made the decision to present the story as Lourdes had revealed it to me, I made only minor comments and occasional interpretations in the text. For the most part it is the voice of Lourdes which speaks directly to us.

Since *Outside the Wall* is a book that was put together by two individuals, it has two authors. We have arranged for 50 percent of the royalties from the sales of the book to go to each of us. To distinguish our separate contributions, we decided to italicize my contribution to the story, with the exception of this introductory chapter and the conclusion, while Lourdes's parts, which constitute most of the book, appear in regular print.

Lourdes was twenty-nine years old when I first met her, and her husband was thirty-two. Those who know and have worked with Lourdes see her as a very distinguished person. People greatly admire her for her dedication to her husband as well as to other inmates and their families. I found Lourdes to be extremely intelligent, if not in strict academic terms, then certainly by her street smarts. Her experience has allowed her to accumulate a large measure of knowledge and insightfulness about individual behavior as well as the workings of social institutions. On occasion I asked her to describe how she best defines herself, and she always replied with the same answer: "I'm just a common person."

This book, then, represents the life story of a "common" Puerto Rican woman who is highly sensitive, caring, and intelligent and who has experienced great changes in her life as she has grown to adulthood. At the broadest level *Outside the Wall* represents the story of one of the hundreds of ordinary people who society knows so little about because it has erected numerous institutional mechanisms and policies to keep them at a distance (as Lourdes would put it: "out of sight, out of mind") and voiceless. This book tells a story that has until now been concealed. Historically, the ideas and interpretations of the dominant social group have been used to convey the stories of people of color and women; that is, the dominant class has given itself the function of presenting the "official" versions of the histories of "these people." This "official body of knowledge," according to anthropologist Clifford Geertz, serves to "maintain the subordination of women, workers, and non-European people by excluding their experiential knowledge of social life from our abstract knowledge of society" (1983, 19).

When people of color and women find ways to tell their stories, however, we see that they differ dramatically from those told by members of the dominant class. The narration of stories such as Lourdes's, when told by the subject him- or herself, revolves around the speaker's subjective descriptions, feelings, thoughts, and meanings of his or her life experiences. These stories, told by "common folks," depict the circumstances confronting these individuals as well as enable them to use their own knowledge—often developed in the course of narration—to improve their chances in society. As Michael McCall and Judith Wittner put it: "because they depend less on concepts grounded in the experiences of social dominant groups and classes, life histories deepen the critique of existing knowledge. They force us to examine our assumptions, incorporate more actors into our models, and generate more inclusive concepts for understanding the actual complexities of social institutions and the processes of social change" (1990, 46).

Thus, like my previous books (Padilla 1985; 1987; 1992), *Outside the Wall* serves as a vehicle for allowing another person from *el barrio*, whose voice has for too long remained muted, to speak for herself. Through the book we will hear Lourdes's voice attempting to reconstruct knowledge about herself as well as about specific elements of the larger society. *Outside the Wall* is built on a perspective illuminated by one feminist historian almost two decades ago: "Refusing to be rendered historically voiceless any longer, women are creating a new history—using our own voices and experiences. We are challenging the traditional concepts of history, of what is 'historically important,' and we are affirming that our everyday lives are history. Using an oral tradition, as old as human memory, we are reconstructing our past" (Gluck 1977, 3).

Although in this book I deal with a single case, I believe it is relevant in a larger context. In a special way Lourdes's story is about the personal changes experienced by an individual as she endeavors to uphold a highly valued and, to her, almost sacred cultural practice: marriage. She is not only interested in keeping her own marriage intact, against great odds, but she has also become an activist dedicated to keeping the families of other prisoners together. In this way she has become an advocate for the rights of Latino and Latina prisoners. Lourdes's narrative of self-transformation and her related commentary demonstrate how subtle social and psychological pressures connect with issues of ethnicity, class membership and consciousness, the conditions facing youth, gender, and political action, categories that have become increasingly interesting to social scientists.

In a larger context this book is concerned in a very fundamental way with the lives of Puerto Rican people in the United States, particularly the situations that second- and now third-generation young women and men face daily. The circumstances of these young people's lives take place within their immediate ethnic and cultural environment, the family and the barrio, as well as within the context of mainstream social institutions and organizations. At the time of this writing interest in Puerto Rican youth has increased substantially among social scientists, the leading areas of inquiry being their school experiences and their involvement in street gangs (Kyle 1989; Padilla 1992).

It is my hope that the remarkable intelligence and articulateness demonstrated by Lourdes will help to illuminate the immense human potential, so often unrealized, which lies outside the normal reach of our social and economic systems. Working with Lourdes has been a humbling experience for me because she is such a vital part of a largely silent and unsung force. When people speak of the courage and honor of the Puerto Rican people they do not necessarily mean people like Lourdes; often they do not even know such people exist. They do exist, however, and for all the daughters and sons of *el barrio* their presence is a reason to rejoice.

I am quite aware of the possible risks involved in doing this work. The major risk concerns the question of a man contributing to the writing of a woman's story. Taking on this project has meant examining critically the vast feminist literature and incorporating some of it into my own way of thinking about human behavior. It has, of course, also meant getting to know Lourdes extremely well, an experience that has greatly enhanced my view of women's courage and commitment to "do the right thing." As Lourdes recounted her story, I became newly informed of a very basic fact: so many people in our society, and in particular women and people of color, live their lives without fulfilling their personal goals. Yet, though they may die without realizing their human potential, they die fighting. At the same time their voices are so muted by their unyielding circumstances that many of us are rarely compelled, even for one moment, to reflect upon their toll. And yet these human beings are not so defeated as it might seem; for the most part they make do with what they have and at times manifest a nobility and courage that is astonishing.

Thus, any risk I took in working with Lourdes has been worth it; I will never be the same again. Have I done a sensible job in presenting Lourdes's story? I am not the one to judge, of course, yet I feel positive about having been able to facilitate a process that has led to the presentation of Lourdes's story. And I am entirely certain that through this process my friend Lourdes has learned a great deal about herself, and for that I am willing to take another risk.

1

Childhood Years and Family Life

As retribution following its defeat in the Spanish-American War, in 1898 Spain's government transferred its colonial rule of Puerto Rico over to Washington politicians. Since the time of the transfer, an act that was carried out without the consent of the Puerto Rican people, severe conditions of unemployment and poverty have been driving Puerto Ricans from their island nation to the United States. With the exception of early groups of migrants who were contracted to work in sugarcane fields in Hawaii and a small number who went to live in Florida, up until the late 1940s Puerto Rican migration was for the most part to the Northeast—in particular, New York City. Then, beginning in the late 1940s, Chicago's reputation as a leading manufacturing and industrial center, where jobs were plentiful, made this midwestern city a new destination point for individuals and families from the island. Puerto Rican migrants by the thousands came to live in the frigid climate of Chicago, joining the ranks of the working class in the physically demanding jobs of manufacturing firms and factories.

On the island itself, sweeping hardships, intensified by depressing eco-

nomic circumstances emerging from American colonialism, were unbearable for most of the island's residents. The U.S. government converted the once multi-crop, agricultural economic system of its new colonial possession into a producer of a single cash-crop, sugarcane. Such a strategy could only lead to massive unemployment, since there were not enough jobs in this solitary industry to employ all available workers.

In the 1940s and 1950s industrialization was introduced not only as an economic initiative that was going to elevate Puerto Rico to the level of a "modern" society but also as a strategy for solving its unemployment catastrophe. Industrial Puerto Rico never developed as planned. Its manufacturing firms were small in size, capable of employing a very limited number of workers. Further, most manufacturing plants were concentrated in particular regions and not in others, thus creating a dual system of regional development and underdevelopment. Thus, like the previous plan for farming a single crop, industrialization severely aggravated the problem of surplus labor, it too leading to a sharp increase in unemployment.

Not capable of providing its own people with work opportunities, in the early 1950s the government of the island—which to this day continues to serve as a satellite structure of the United States, and which has, as expected, been highly supportive of political, economic, and social policies and programs initiated in Washington—turned to migration as a solution to its immediate economic problems. Organizations made up of dissatisfied workers emerged during this period, demanding changes in the way of life into which they, as members of the Puerto Rican working class, had been forced. Enormous fear of potential workers' revolts and insurrections was deeply felt by the insular government. It reasoned that, by "flying" surplus labor to the American mainland, the potential for such uprisings would be significantly curtailed.

Indeed, Puerto Rico's government began sponsoring and promoting emmigration, selling the American mainland, in particular, as the "promised land." Relying on the government's projections and out of desperation, Puerto Ricans began leaving their beloved island. One count has it that by 1960 a total of 612,574 Puerto Ricans left the San Juan airport for a

region in the United States (Senior and Watkins 1966). Already by 1970
78,963 Puerto Ricans (a 100 percent increase from the previous decade)
were calling Chicago home, even if many saw it as a temporary or secondary
home (Padilla 1987).

Accommodation into a new society and culture has always been a major
challenge for immigrants the world over. Family members and friends who
are already established in a new place often assist immigrants with this
process of adjustment. This was the case with Lourdes's parents, who came
from different towns in Puerto Rico to live in Chicago in the late 1950s.
For these two relatives who had earlier settled in Chicago came to play this
important role, providing them with lodging and particularly assistance in
securing employment.

My mother arrived in Chicago before my father. The year she
came was 1957, maybe 1958. She wasn't even twenty years old
when she came to live with one of her sisters, who was already
settled here. Her sister was married and had her own family. It was
her sister who wrote to inform my mother of different job oppor-
tunites in Chicago. My mother immediately began thinking about
coming to live here.

At that time her mother, father, brothers, and sisters lived in
Puerto Rico, and things were bad. People in general were having a
difficult time making ends meet. Her plans included working to
help out her family as she could. She knew of so many other people
who had been sent by their parents to come and work here or came
voluntarily to sacrifice for the family. This practice was becoming
almost a tradition among the working class of the island, because
everyone was in the same boat. There was a great deal of suffering
throughout Puerto Rico at that time.

This and other similar information I gathered from my mother's
conversations with my father and friends who visited the house.
She never discussed these things with her children. I suspect that
the experience was so devastating that she didn't want us to have

any history of it. As an adult, I have come to know people who have shared with me their experiences of trying to survive in Puerto Rico, and they went through the same thing as my mother.

In any event coming to Chicago also presented my mother with the opportunity to escape her parents' stern system of upbringing. Although she was already a young woman, she was not permitted to do anything alone. She could not date or go out with other young men. So, when the opportunity presented itself she took it. She still lives in Chicago, though she has gone back many times [to Puerto Rico] to visit with her parents and brothers and sisters.

Once in Chicago my mother lived with my aunt until she was married. She found a job and also helped her sister with house chores. In addition, she assumed the responsibility of taking care of my cousins, who were small then. All of these things were part of her responsibility as a member of the family. It was expected that, if a person comes to live in someone's house, even when the person is just a friend of the family, the person is supposed to contribute to the welfare of that person's family by helping out. Since my aunt had three children at that time, my mother thought that taking care of them was the least she could do. My mother used to tell us stories about my cousins from the times she was caring for them.

My father, on the other hand, was born and raised in Puerto Rico, and after serving in the [U.S.] army he decided to come to the United States and live with his brothers and sisters who were already here. He was drafted into the service. He had no choice. In the 1950s many of the island's young people were drafted into the service. He had some relatives here, so after he finished his military term he decided to come to Chicago to stay with them.

Like my mother, my father's decision to come to live in Chicago was motivated by the lack of job opportunities in Puerto Rico. Although he was a veteran, he was just another worker looking for essentially the same kind of work as everybody else. He was not given any preference as an ex-soldier; after all, there weren't any jobs in the first place. He came to Chicago to work, and that he has done. He has not stopped working; he is still going.

My mother and father met here. And they were married here. My father is ten years older than my mother. When they got married my mother was twenty-three, and he was thirty-three. They did not date very long. I think they went out less than a year before they decided to marry. Unfortunately, this would be a reason for their divorce later on.

Anyway, the way they met was also unusual. My father, who knew my aunt and her family, had gone to her house where my mother was living. There he saw a picture of my mom, and he asked my aunt who the person in the picture was. My aunt told him that it was her sister who had just come from Puerto Rico. They were introduced by my aunt. Later my aunt set up a secret date so they could meet. After that they continued meeting and talking, and one thing led to another, and they got married.

From what I can remember I think my mother attended school in Puerto Rico through the ninth grade. I don't really know why she stopped going to school. My mother did not talk much about school. She preferred telling us stories about when she was growing up as a tomboy. Her stories were about growing up around boys all the time. She used to tell us how my grandfather, who was very strict, would tell her to act like a girl. My mother used to love when the cars would get stuck in the mud, and she would run out of the house to push them. Apparently, girls were not supposed to be doing those things. Certainly, from the way my mother is today it's so difficult for me to see her as a tomboy.

I wish my mother had told us about her days in school. I wonder if she liked school or not. It would have been good to learn about her friends. When you're in school you always make friends—I never knew this part of my mother. To me this information was important because it would have given me an idea of the things she went through. When we were young and wanted to do some things she would say, "I went through all of that, so, therefore, you don't have to repeat it." We would look at her and tell her: "What? You never told us anything of what you did or didn't do." But, you know, if you spend time around older parents, they all use the same line: "I was coming when you were going"—and that was their way of telling you that you don't have to do those things because they did them, and look what happened to them.

Except for my oldest brother, who is not even a year older than I am, we were born in Puerto Rico. We lived in Chicago, but my mother would go to Puerto Rico when it was time to give birth so my grandmother could take care of her. She would go there for that special event. My mother wanted to be there with my grandmother so she could take care of her.

It's strange because normally Latino men are very controlling. They are perceived as "machos" who force their wives to play subservient roles. My father wasn't. Today he would be defined as a liberated man. My father was very open-minded. He believed very strongly in equality. My father would give the shirt off his back for us. My mother was the one who laid down the law. And I think she was the one who wanted to go to Puerto Rico to give birth. My father always agreed.

I've spoken to other women and asked them if they went through the same experience, and they all said no. They told me they wanted to go to Puerto Rico to give birth because they wanted to be with their mothers, but their husbands said no and that that was going to be the way it was. That attitude was very typical: "No, you're not going to do that"—and that was that.

My aunt was here in Chicago, and she could have easily helped out, but my mother wanted to go to Puerto Rico. She believed that only her mother could give her the care and commitment required by that occasion. So, she went to Puerto Rico to be with her mother, not once but twice. It happened for me and my sister, who is younger than me.

Puerto Rican newcomers arrived in Chicago with a strong work ethic, a traditional commitment to working hard and being productive. Like many other immigrants who settled in Chicago, Lourdes's mother and father became factory workers and were highly regarded for their dedication to their jobs. Though their jobs were physically taxing and low paying, Lourdes used their experiences to develop a clear idea of the importance of work. Even when the work is difficult and exploitative, for Lourdes it has come to represent a major element of a person's identity. Lourdes understands work as the means of being self-sufficient, at least of distancing oneself from the public aid office.

For as long as I can remember my mother and father were always working. The two of them worked in factory jobs, but they were always working in a job—they were not without work. My mother stopped working during the time when the three of us were babies. We were all about a year or so apart, but after we were a little bigger she went back to work. Our parents simply needed to work to care for us. They always wanted to give us everything we needed, and for that they needed two checks.

My mother had to go on welfare after she divorced my father because there were the three of us, and she wanted to stay home to continue taking care of us. After a few years she returned to work. To this day she is still working.

From my mother's experience with work I learned that, when it was my turn to go out there to the work world, I would be working all the time. As far back as I can remember, I had come to understand the importance of being able to work all the time. I made up my mind never to rely on government funding to sustain me. Not that government assistance is bad; there are those who need it, and the fact that the government makes it available to them is great. But I have known that, as long as I was capable of going out to work, I was not going to stay home.

Again, it's not that my mother liked staying home—she had to.

She was caring for three children growing up. I learned that a person or family can barely survive from what they receive in public assistance. The budget of this family is extremely tight. The person has to be very careful about what to buy. I remember times when we wanted to buy candy or ice cream, but we couldn't. So, this woman, this mother, has to restrict herself; she can't give her children what they want. For her there is no enjoyment in life. And, of course, that woman lives under enormous stress. I made up my mind that this was not going to be me. I remember thinking that I wanted to work because, if I wanted to splurge, then I could do it and not have to worry. I didn't want to have to say, "Well, it's not the time of the month to buy extra things."

Basically, I came to understand the importance of being able to work because I did not want to be dependent on anyone. I wanted to be able to survive and make ends meet on my own. To this day it bothers me to have to ask for help at times. People say that there's nothing wrong with asking for help, but I've grown up thinking and knowing that I want to be independent. My goal was to depend on myself. Since I've always worked, I've made my choices and decisions.

In fact, when I was twelve my brother and I were already working. We got jobs in the city's Summer Youth Employment Program. This was our first real job. We did not simply sit down and say, "Well, we would rather be in the streets trying to hustle some money." No, we wanted to work. And when we got paid we would come home and give our checks to our mother. She, in turn, would give us a couple of dollars to spend.

I didn't mind giving my mother my earnings because they represented some help. I'm glad that my brother and I were able to help. My mother needed the assistance. Actually, we used to think that she spent what we gave her. But when it was time to return to school my mother would come and tell us, "Okay, we are going shopping." And we were very surprised, since we thought there was no money to buy school supplies or clothes. My mother would tell us, "You guys gave me your money, and this is for you." In essence, she had saved the money we gave her during the summer. There were times when she needed to buy something and did use some of the money, but the other times she kept the money to clothe us.

From a very young age we all learned that, if we want something, we have to earn it. My mother wasn't one that would say, "You can have whatever you want—it's okay with me." I'll never forget the time when, after I had noticed that everyone in school was wearing makeup, I asked my mother to buy me some, along with powder. She said to me, "When you work and earn your own pay you buy it." She wanted to show us that, if we want something, we're going to have to work for it. At that time I used to think that it was kind of mean; after all, what I wanted only cost one dollar. But the theory behind what she was showing us was that not everything comes easy. You have to work for it. And when you work for something you come to appreciate it more. You protect it and cherish it.

As a matter of fact, my sister has instilled that philosophy in the minds of her children. One time when I was visiting her in St. Louis, where she now lives, I saw her doing exactly what our mother had taught us. My sister would give her children an allowance of a dollar to go to the store. They could only spend that dollar that she had given them. And this last time when I was visiting it hurt me because I wanted to buy other things for them, but I couldn't because my sister always said not to. The idea is that they have one dollar, and mom or dad are not going to add additional spending money, so they have to learn to do with what they have.

In Puerto Rican culture the family takes pride in raising its children. In this regard the family is defined in its traditional extended form: it is composed of parents, grandparents, brothers, sisters, cousins, and godparents. Friends who are close to the family are considered godparents (comadres *or* com-

padres) and are treated as family; These individuals take care of the children. Using babysitters outside the family is avoided, but when children were looked after by non-family members these individuals become intimate with the family and are considered part of the family circle.

Lourdes's parents made enormous sacrifices to raise their children by themselves. Among the things they agreed to do was to work different shifts so that one parent was always at home. The only time Lourdes and her sister and brother were not with their parents occurred between shifts, when one parent was going to work and the other was coming home. For this short period of time Lourdes and her sister and brother were cared for by a woman who was considered family.

Even though our parents were always working, we were never that apart from them because they worked different shifts. They worked different hours so they could be with us. My mother was working nights, while my father worked days. It was only during a particular time of the day when the two of them were away, usually for two to three hours, like around three to six in the afternoon, that we were not with them. That was usually the time we were taken to a babysitter. This was a major sacrifice on the part of my parents. What they were doing taught us how much they cared for us, how genuinely concerned they were for us. They didn't want to just go out of the house and leave us with a babysitter to raise us. They didn't want us to feel like they were abandoning us for work. We realized that they needed to go to work, but by the same token they didn't want to communicate the idea, "Well, we have to go to work, and you guys have to go to the babysitter." They believed that, since we were their children, it was their responsibility to bring us up. And for them work was not going to stand in the way.

I remember my mother taking us to our babysitter, who was this little old lady; actually, she was much bigger than her husband. We used to call her Big Mama. She would lay down the law in her house too. But to us Big Mama and her husband were our grandparents because our own were in Puerto Rico, and at that time we were little and didn't know them. I think they also treated us like part of their family. They treated us very special. We were not just kids that they were looking after but kids who were just as important as their own.

We really loved Big Mama. She was really good. Although I was very young when she took care of us—I was probably five or six years old—I still remember her very clearly. And that's because she was really special.

I remember that every time my father dropped us off Big Mama would be standing by the door waiting for us. She would grab us and give us a big hug, and, since we were so tiny, she would grab all three of us at the same time and tells us in Spanish, "Vengan mis niños a su casa" (Come, my kids, to your home). She would make sure that if we wanted something to eat there would be a snack already prepared. And, as we were growing up, she made sure that when we came to her house we would do our homework before sitting down to watch television. She was great—a special member of our family. I think she thought of us as special members of her family.

Lourdes's parents' arrival in Chicago in the late 1950s coincided with the increasing growth of the Westown/Humboldt Park communities into the largest area of Puerto Rican settlement in the city. Known by local residents as "Division Street" (Padilla 1987), these two communities, which are a few miles northwest of downtown, are adjacently to one another and are considered as one. It was here that Lourdes's family eventually came to live.

Because many of the residents were newcomers who shared the same ethnic background and working-class status a spirit of collectivism developed among Division Street residents. Nurturance and support were seen as natural forms of behavior in the neighborhood, and there was no minimizing the value of interdependence upon which neighborhood relations were based. People lived within relationships that were extremely closely knit and enduring.

Within each individual there was a tremendous sense of community, and each carried this out in public. "Este es nuestro barrio" *(This is our neighborhood) was a popular slogan often expressed by local residents. Much of life on Division Street mirrored that which the migrants had left behind in their hometowns and villages of Puerto Rico. In particular, people persistently sought ways to develop and maintain an atmosphere of trust and fraternity among themselves as* familia y vecinos *(family and neighbors).*

For as long as I can remember we lived in the Humboldt Park area—what we call Division Street. Division Street is where the major cultural activities and structures of the Puerto Rican community were found. Like we used to say when we were youngsters, "Division Street was what was happening."

We lived in a different neighborhood before moving to Division Street. My brother remembers living on the South Side, near Sacramento and Roosevelt [streets]. I vaguely remember that because I was very young. But I do remember my father's youngest brother getting married there. I still remember the church. The few memories I still have of that neighborhood make it seem so different from the way it is now. People would sit on benches without having to worry about being mugged or anything. That has changed totally now.

When my brother was eight or nine we moved to the north side, to Division Street. I think we came to live here because things were getting really bad in our old neighborhood. It was changing, and there were always frictions and fights between the black boys and Puerto Rican boys. So, my parents decided to leave. I'm not saying that my parents have anything against other racial groups, but from their conversations it was clear that they felt they weren't safe there anymore. They wanted to move where there were more Puerto Ricans. The fact that Division Street was emerging as a Puerto Rican neighborhood appealed to them a great deal. They believed that it would be more appropriate to raise their children among others of their kind. They felt that in a Puerto Rican neighborhood everyone knew how to deal with one another. Because we share the same culture, my parents assumed that, even in cases of friction, we would have the know-how for resolving them. And, since my parents did not speak English very well, they had difficulties understanding things people said to them in our other neighborhood.

People say that my neighborhood is terrible, but I'm glad to say that people can grow up and make something out of their life. I grew up here, and, though I married a gang member, we've come a long way, and we've learned that life teaches us a lot and we can turn things around. I would get very upset to hear people put down this neighborhood. There were the teachers in school who hated Division Street, the very same neighborhood where they taught. They were always making smart remarks about the 'hood and the people in it. Since I was young, I guess I couldn't understand why they would say those things. I knew that there were problems, but I still didn't see things as bad as they made them seem. Now that I'm much older, I see things differently. However, since I'm still here, I guess I must like it.

When I was young I had this perception of Humboldt Park that this neighborhood, my neighborhood, was the extent of life. As far as I was concerned, this was it. I imagined that beyond this point, that beyond this area, there wasn't much more. Obviously, I knew there were other neighborhoods, parks, and schools, but I couldn't see anything other than the local store, the local grammar school, and the high school on the corner. Division Street was much of what I knew.

There was this older store owned by an older American couple but which is no longer there. The kids from the neighborhood came to know the couple very well. I'm sure this old couple saw us in our mother's stomach. They saw us as babies. They knew us from the very beginning. We had this special respect for them, like if they were part of our family. To them we were not only customers; we were the kids from the neighborhood, their kids. It was special.

When I was in grammar school every day after school I would stop at the store along with the other kids. There were times when we would just stand in front and hang out. We would talk and gossip. Other times we would go inside and buy candy for a few pennies. Or sometimes we would go inside the store to browse around to see if any new candy had come in. I used to go there every day. Everyone stopped there from school. It was our hangout place. Every neighborhood where there is a grammar school you can find a store like the one that existed in ours. And kids adopt it as theirs.

And then there was a store owned by a Puerto Rican man—the store was very Puerto Rican. People would go and buy what they needed to cook with: their seasonings and their tomatoes and their lettuce. This is where people went to buy their rice and beans and all the other foods from the island. And you could go there and get your Spanish newspaper as well as catching up on the latest gossip because people were always standing outside and inside talking about the goings-on in the neighborhood, in their lives, in Puerto Rico. For some people the store was a very important source of information. They learned where to find a cheaper apartment or car, what happened with so-and-so and why so-and-so moved out or why so-and-so got divorced.

I remember the owner of the store as always being kind and caring. He extended credit to his customers. You could go there, buy some items, and say, "I'll pay you next week" (*apuntalo*), and the owner would say, "Okay." Of course, the credit sheet [the list on which debts are noted] for every customer would be very long. Buying on credit was one way of living and surviving.

My neighborhood was a world within itself. People could live here without having to have contact with the outside world. Why should they? Everything they needed was here. And, since we were mostly Latinos, it was like a big family. Because my mother didn't drive, and because of the fact that we attended school in the neighborhood and we were involved in church, there wasn't really much of anything else. That's what I used to think. Maybe in the summer we would go to the park, or my father would take us to Kiddyland. Later, after my mother divorced my father and remarried, my stepfather would take us out because he had friends, and in the summer we would go out to Lake Geneva in Wisconsin. I remember that we would drive to Lake Geneva and see a world that was totally different. This was the world of country life and living. I used to like the country. There were horses and cows. The air smelled different. Everything seemed so free.

I couldn't help but compare what I would see outside of Chicago to Humboldt Park. Where we lived was not very safe. On those few times when we went to the park with our parents we had to be careful at all times because the gangs were at war with one another. And then all of a sudden there is this environment where you could run around freely and play and go into the water. It was quite different. And, as a child, I used to wish that we could live there. But it was only a dream. It is not like I told my mother, "Let's move there," but, as working-class people, we simply could not afford to travel to many places outside the neighborhood, and when we did have a chance to go somewhere it didn't matter how the place was—we were always impressed by it. I see these places today and wonder how could I have reacted to them the way I did then. They do not look attractive; they seem so lifeless.

But my neighborhood was my neighborhood, and that's where I was and presumably was going to stay. There is no denying that neighborhood people were poor. This didn't matter to me because we were all in the same boat. We weren't any poorer or richer than other folks. We were all pretty much the same, and we weren't trying to outdo the other. I couldn't see any difference.

My mother always pointed out to us that, no matter how poor we were, if we were good with other people, that was how you became rich. What she was telling us was to always be proud of who we are, not to let anyone make us feel inferior just because we may not have what they have in terms of material possessions or even in education attainment. I have never felt ashamed for not having or owning what others possess. My dignity is what makes me rich and makes me feel good. Being good and fair to other people was my riches. I learned these wonderful lessons from my mother. I'm glad that she taught us those values because I have lived some very difficult times, and her lessons have carried me forward.

And, although the people in the neighborhood were poor, they treated each other with respect. People in the neighborhood treated one another as a family. Everybody knew each other. There was a lot of caring. There was a sharing of commitment for individuals and families. People knew everyone who moved in and out of the neighborhood. When something would happen there was always someone there to take care of it or to address the particular situation. It was known that people could rely on their neighbors. If you had a fight with the kid next door, the kid's mother would come over and work things out with your mother. When we were kids it was difficult doing things in the neighborhood because, if people saw you, they would immediately bring the news over to your house. Missing school when you were expected to be in class—that wonderful custom that so many kids try at least once in a lifetime—was a very risky thing to do. Dare you be seen by someone who knew your family, you were sure to get a beating from your mother or father because they would learn about it.

For Lourdes straying outside Division Street did not always produce positive outcomes. During visits to areas such as downtown Chicago she experienced directly the racial tension and antagonism of U.S. society. Individuals reacted to Lourdes and her family, as Puerto Ricans, with much racial indifference or even disdain. Lourdes and her family were made to feel like intruders, people who had stepped outside their boundaries. In other words, Lourdes experienced the unpleasant feeling associated with the question, stated openly or not: What are these Puerto Ricans doing here? These encounters reminded Lourdes and her family that, as Puerto Ricans, they were targets of racial prejudice and discrimination. Instead of succumbing to these threats, Lourdes and her family used them to further strengthen their ethnicity. Their commitment to the goodness and worthiness of their Puerto Rican ethnic tradition was reinforced by these acts of racial injustice.

Going downtown to State Street was a big deal. We had a tradition in our family that, in the winter, my cousin or aunt would take us downtown to window-shop. We used to go there to see the Christmas tree and to walk down State Street, to ride the train. It was fun. We would go to the store and see merchandise I knew I never would buy.

I also met with people there who were outright nasty. They would be all dressed up in fancy clothes, basically with their noses up in the air and walking and looking at you like, "What is this Puerto Rican kid doing here, walking downtown, out of her neighborhood?" I didn't care about their attitude because I was out to have a nice time and I thought I had every right to be there just like they did.

Going downtown was extremely hard on my mother because to this day she doesn't speak very much English. If she tried to communicate in a store when buying something, she always tried to ask for assistance. I could always see people being nasty and making fun of her. Although we would translate for her, I could still notice the pain and embarrassment she was suffering. My mother would tell us in Spanish, *"Esa persona es tan ignorante"* (That person is so ignorant).

My mother used these occasions to remind us about the importance of not letting people downgrade us. Since she couldn't answer back because of her language difference, she would still tell us to remain unmoved about what others say about us. She's very firm and strong when it comes to having people respect you. If she doesn't like something, she lets the person know. She is like that to this day. If she goes into a restaurant and the food is cold, she immediately tells the waiter, "My food should be hot—I'm paying for it." She doesn't accept anything that she's not supposed to get.

If my mother walks into a store and people begin to follow her around, she simply walks out. Even if that is the only store where she could find what she's looking for, she will walk away. This is another of her ways for dealing with people who treat her rude.

I find myself doing that sometimes, though I think I'm more outspoken. Before I used to accept things; hardly ever did I fight for anything. But not anymore. I've gone into stores, and people have followed me, and I find this very annoying, so I've walked right out.

A series of events contributed to the transformation of Lourdes's neighborhood into a site saturated with much intergang rivalry among youths. Residents who had lived in the neighborhood for a long time began moving away. Many returned to Puerto Rico, while others went to live with a son or daughter in a different neighborhood. Others simply moved their family to what they believed to be safer neighborhoods.

Puerto Rican youngsters from the second generation, who were in their teens a few years earlier, started turning to the gang in search of the identity, dignity, and monetary possessions they believed the larger society had denied them. As a teenager, Lourdes too was a member of this generation of young people who were changing the character of Division Street.

As the years went on, things began changing in the neighborhood. It started getting a little bit worse. Some of the older residents, the older Puerto Rican residents who seemed to have lived there for years, began to move out because they didn't have any more kids. They decided to go live with a son or daughter who was married. Some retired and finally went home to Puerto Rico. For this last group the dream of going home to their beloved island was finally accomplished. They came to Chicago to work and to return someday; they did, though many were old. Others went back to Puerto Rico because they felt that the education system here was terrible and their kids could be better educated in Puerto Rico.

There was my neighbor from next door who decided to go back to Puerto Rico. That was hard for me, my sister, and brother because the daughters and sons were close with us. We were best of friends. Then the neighbor next to them, with whom we were very close too, bought a house and moved. The people on the first floor from where we lived left the neighborhood as well.

All of this happened within one single year. It was like removing the foundation of a house. You knew that the walls would crumble because they could not support themselves. It's funny that I had thought this way at that time since I was so young. But that's exactly how I saw what was happening. It was like an exchange taking place: the older people who had been there for many, many years were moving out, and younger people were coming in. This kind of exchange always spells some trouble.

Many of the young people who moved in were involved in gangs. I really believe that it was gang activity that made the people start moving out. In my view gang activities changed everything. The gangs were spreading throughout the neighborhood. There were the Cobras and Disciples in the same general area, while a few blocks away were the Jivers and Spanish Lords. The kids were now fourteen or fifteen, and they were becoming members of the various neighborhood gangs. It seemed like there were thousands of these young people. They were members of my generation.

It is my belief that the coming of this generation of teenagers is responsible for the visibility of gang activity in our neighborhood. I remember that, while there were gangs before, you sometimes didn't notice them. But with the coming of all these kids it was quite obvious that gangs were developing into large organizations. We became aware that they were spreading throughout the neighborhood searching for drug-dealing markets. Gangs were creating their drug-dealing corners and making sure that oppositional gangs did not take over them. So, there developed a group of guys on that corner and this other corner who were saying, "I'm not moving out of here, this is my 'hood." What finally happened was that one gang began selling this product on this particular corner, another was selling the same product on another corner, and customers were going to only one. Before long the gangs who were competing for the same clientele started fighting one another. And, of course, that is when the shootings and killings began. That's when people said, "This is not for me—I want out of here." And they began moving out of the neighborhood and going elsewhere.

My family moved out to a different area in the neighborhood, but after getting married I moved right back. I feel like I belong here. Even now, as I sit down with my coworkers, who know my experience of grief and pain, they ask me: "Why don't you move out? Why are you still there since his [my husband's] friends live in the neighborhood?" To me this is my neighborhood. I feel safe here. I don't think I can be this safe someplace else. Here I know everyone. When I walk down the street and people see me coming they say: "Oh, yeah, that's Lourdes. She's Doña Juanita's daughter." I'm very aware of the fact that many bad things happen as well, but I just feel comfortable.

Another thing is that I'm seeing that the people are coming back, and the youth that grew up here are buying property and reestablishing their roots. Not far from here are a couple of brothers who used to be gangbangers; they now own their buildings.

Further down from these guys are four brothers who just bought their own house. That makes me feel good because they could have bought elsewhere. They decided to stay here and help to rebuild the neighborhood.

It's funny because I know these guys. I saw them growing up and doing the things that most kids were doing in those days. They used to write on the walls of buildings, but, now that they are home owners, they are making sure that nobody does this to their property. So, in essence they can help out a lot because, by enforcing the law of the neighborhood as they see things now, they're ensuring that their property is well maintained. This behavior makes other people in the neighborhood become more watchful of what they own.

Although Lourdes's parents were born and raised in Puerto Rico, their plan was to raise their children in Chicago. Any prospects of returning to their homeland were clouded by memories of the depressing economic conditions they had left behind. They understood the meaning of growing up during conditions of limited work opportunities, and they were not about to repeat the lives of their youth. In addition, for Lourdes's mother the city of Chicago represented a safe haven for escaping the unyielding strictness around which she had been brought up.

My mother quickly adapted to life in Chicago, and she didn't want to go back and live with the family the way it was. She had nine brothers and sisters in her immediate family and some very strict parents. My grandparents were very strict. I still remember that my mother, even when she was in her forties and we were visiting in Puerto Rico, would not even smoke in front of my grandfather. She wouldn't say a bad word in front of him. None of my uncles would drink in front of him. They were brought up to respect their elders. My grandfather would tell my uncles, "You're never too old to be slapped." I think my mother wanted to get away from the restriction. She needed air to breathe, and apparently she found it here in Chicago.

While Lourdes's parents came to Chicago to work, attending and succeeding in school was the primary goal they assigned to their children. Lourdes's parents believed that education would enable their children to succeed in life. In their minds education was the "great equalizer," the weapon to be used for overcoming the racial and sexual prejudice and discrimination that tend to prevent some individuals and groups from realizing their talents. Lourdes's parents reasoned too that factory work went to those who did not get far in school—their daughters and son were certain not to fall into this trap.

Throughout elementary school Lourdes was right on track in terms of fulfilling her parents' vision. She was an excellent student—in her view, one of the best in her classes.

School for me was a very joyful experience. I was a teacher's pet. I would always do my homework and sit at my desk quietly and paying attention to what the teacher was saying. Some of my classmates would always talk and do things they were not supposed to do. I used to look at them and think that they were not going to learn anything, that they were not going to amount to much. I used to think things like "Why don't they just listen and do what the teachers tell them?" I wasn't really criticizing them, but this was the kind of student I was. School to me was important, and we needed to take advantage of it.

Because of the way I was as a student, the teacher would always call on me to answer questions. Sometimes I didn't answer because, although I knew the answer, I expected one of my classmates to say: "Oh, just ask Lourdes. She knows everything." This was very hard for me.

I wanted to be a teacher. I used to play school on the back porch of the building where we lived. I would gather the younger children from the neighborhood and teach them the alphabet and how to count. I used to teach them how to work with numbers. It was a lot of fun. This experience made me feel like I was in control and that I was teaching and helping someone who could use my knowledge. The kids loved it too.

Since I was so involved in doing my schoolwork, the teachers pushed and stimulated me. I was convinced—I really believed in my mind—that I would one day succeed. I was so sure that I would become something. It sounded so simple: I will become something as long as I kept going to school and was doing well. In fact, while I was in eighth grade, I was recruited to participate in a program at Clemente High School. This was a special French language program for eighth-graders who were doing well in school. We would receive two credits of high school work for taking French classes two times a week.

I think that there were two or three other students from my school in the French program. I liked the fact that I was one of them because it showed that my efforts had paid off. I was in eighth grade, yet I was attending high school classes to earn high school credits. It turned out to be a very good experience. I received a B+ in the class. We learned to do little skits in French and things like that.

I liked my teachers very much. They always told me that they saw something different in me from the other kids. They paid close attention to my feelings. If I came to school sad, they would ask me what was wrong. There was a special bond; they were really good teachers. I will always remember them.

History and English were my favorite subjects. I liked history because I was always curious—I wanted to know how things came about. Then my curiosity would increase when I would open a book and there would be an account of Christopher Columbus and how he discovered America and the three ships and stuff like that.

My mind would go back into time, and I wondered if it all really happened like that.

I also liked my English class because I enjoyed writing. I have always liked doing essays and book reports. I liked being able to put my ideas on paper, having the opportunity to express myself, to say what I want to say and the way I want to say it. Writing to me was important because of the way I grew up: my mother always told me to speak my mind. She always reminded us that no one can take your freedom of expression. My writing assignments in school allowed me to express myself; they allowed me to say what I felt. For example, one thing that teachers always want students to do when school begins is to write about summer experiences. I enjoyed being able to write about the things I did and how it all was. Sometimes I would go into a fantasy world and dream up how I would love to live.

What seemed like a smooth path to educational success for Lourdes also was filled with a great deal of emotional stress and frustration. Lourdes was having to carry out her assigned school role within a context of severe parental control. Like in many other Puerto Rican families, Lourdes's mother was extremely protective and dominating. Her mother's major concern was to make Lourdes into an obedient person, a person who would listen and follow only her mother's directions. Above all, this meant not having close friends, since, in her mother's view, they could influence or shape a contrasting way of thinking and behavior.

In other words, it was expected that Lourdes's character was to be molded by the ideas and ways of thinking of her mother, who was now her sole guardian. Lourdes was expected to harness any inner feelings of rebellion or contempt; they were okay as long as they were not expressed outwardly. Lourdes's mother felt that her responsibility was to make her children into the most all-around "perfect adults" possible. As a result, Lourdes did not have much of a private life, living as she did according to her mother's aspirations.

I didn't have many friends in grade school. Some of the kids used to think that I was conceited. It used to hurt to know that they thought of me that way, because I wasn't. I have always thought of myself as someone who liked to help people. But in their minds I was this little girl who believed she was too good to be with them. In reality, I simply felt like there were other things to do than hanging out and being a troublemaker.

Another reason for not having very close friends was that my mom was really strict. After the separation between my father and mother she became very overprotective. I guess it was because she never wanted to give my father the opportunity to say she wasn't a good mother. So, she always made sure we were home by a certain time. She used to clock us on our way home from school. It was required that we go home right after school. Her policy was that, since school let out at 2:30, we had to be home by 2:35. In her mind the distance between school and home could be easily walked in five minutes at most.

There was one incident involving my brother that I will never forget. My brother had a good friend who invited him to the park after school one day. The friend assured my brother that they would be home early. My brother, who was always easygoing, agreed to go. So, they went to the park and started playing on the swings. And they didn't realize that time had passed by. Two hours later my mother was frantic. She called the police, and they did a neighborhood search and found my brother playing on the swings. My brother was scared because he didn't know what he had done wrong. At home he was crying. My mother was relieved, but then she sat him down and told him: "Don't you ever do that again. We didn't know where you were, you're supposed to come home straight after school."

Then there were the Sundays when we would go to the show to see a movie but still couldn't get away from our mother. It was that my sister, brother, and I and some friends would get together and go to the Tiffin, a movie theater which is no longer standing today. We would do this basically every Sunday for a long time. And my mother would go to the show to pick us up. Most of the time that was kind of embarrassing because everyone else was going home on the bus, and here was my mother standing outside the theater waiting for us. Only after a while did she begin allowing us to go home on the bus.

I didn't care for these rules. I wanted to be able to spend time with friends. I wanted to sleep over at their houses and have sleepovers at mine. But I couldn't do those things because my mother, as a single parent, was very protective.

My mother's controlling approach was especially afflictive to me. Since I was the oldest female, I was expected to behave according to the rules she laid out. I had to set the example. When I did manage to have close friends and a boyfriend my mother was against it. When it came to boyfriends it was out of the question for her.

She was raising us the very same way she had been raised by her parents. Being obedient and respectful were seen as the highest and most virtuous acts. My cousins stayed in school and got degrees—this was a way of making sure you became something that was really important. This was the payoff of her system of domination. As far as my mother was concerned, education for all of us was her main objective too. As a mother, she wanted to feel she was doing a good job even though she was doing it alone.

I don't fault her for it. This was the life she knew. And, apparently, she didn't see a need to change it for her children; after all, that way of life had worked for her and many others.

We couldn't hardly go anywhere. If we did anything it was as a family. I guess I could see her point: she was trying to protect us as much as possible, but she overprotected us. If she had given us a little room to breathe and to experience life a little bit more, instead of falling in love with one person and marrying him, maybe I wouldn't have gotten married so young. It used to hurt when me and my sister would say that we liked a boy, because my mother would always say: "No, you are crazy. That cannot be. You don't know what you are talking about." I was expecting her to be more open-minded, to sit us down and tell us: "Oh, you like that boy? Well, that's nice. Let him come to see you, and we would look at it as a form of friendship." Instead, she would not hear about us having boyfriends. She always thought that we were going to do something bad, like running away. So, I got married when I did because I had to get out.

After I got married, and after seeing what happened between me and my husband, my mother began to change. It was interesting because here came my little sister liking this guy and several others before she got married. With the guy that she married she was allowed to go on a school trip to Florida with him. I couldn't even go to the show by myself, and here was my sister going with some guy across the United States. So, I guess what happened with me—my marriage and the problems—my mother decided to be more flexible with my sister by giving her more choices.

Her strictness is also responsible for the fact that we were not very close as mother and daughter. I was close with my mother, but not enough to tell her about my insecurities, about my feelings, and about particular ideas that I had developed about some things. If I would have had the opportunity to communicate with my mother and tell her how I felt about certain things, I would have told her that I didn't like certain people that came to the house, or this or that. I was never able to tell her anything—not because my mother didn't give me the opportunity, but because I saw her with such a character of seriousness and strictness. I see kids today with their mothers, and it looks like they can tell them everything. I didn't feel I could tell my mother anything.

So, I grew up with a lot of feelings inside of me. To this day I still don't want to talk about some things. It is only now through our meetings and discussions that I have been able to open up and share with you some of these things. But when I was young, not being able to tell her my feelings, I ended up crying all the time. Now, as an adult, I think that maybe I should have gone to someone, that maybe I should have told someone how I felt and what was happening to me. It bothers me now because I feel I shouldn't have kept these feelings and pains inside of myself.

It was my mother who I wanted to go to, but I couldn't. Her character was very serious. "Things have to be this way," she would always say. Basically, she would give us anything. If we received good grades in school, she would reward us by taking us to Puerto Rico or New York. But one thing we never did, that I thought was very important, was to play. She would never jump into bed with us and play.

What is so terrible is that, instead of playing with us, and because of her seriousness, she resorted to a system of retribution. In particular, she employed the practice of physical punishment. For as long as I can remember she would hit us. That was her way of disciplining us. I remember that I would run the other way when I saw her coming with the whip, this black belt she had. Running away used to make her angry because it made her run after me. She was beginning to get old and hated running. But once she caught us she would hit us twice as hard.

This particular time—I don't remember exactly what I did—she came after me, and, as I tried to run, she took a swing at me, and the belt hit me across the face. She got very worried. I'll never forget this incident. My whole face burned and bubbled up. And I had to go to school the next day like this. She tried to keep me from going to school, but I wanted to go. I wanted my teachers to see me like I was. It was weird because I wanted my teachers to see me so they would tell her something, but on the other hand I was scared. I didn't want them to do anything that would harm her; after all, this was my mother.

So, I went to school, and the minute I walked into the classroom the teacher had a major fit and took me to the main office. The principal saw me, and he immediately called the police. I was crying. They were asking me, "Who did this to you? You have to tell us," so I finally told them that it was my mother but that it was an accident. They called my mother in, and she started crying. She hugged me, and I hugged her. She felt really bad. What hurt me the most was the guilt on her face. She had this look on her face that said: "I already apologized to you. I told you not to run when I'm trying to hit you." I felt really bad because what I saw in her was a look that clearly said: "I didn't mean it. Oh, I'm really sorry. You know that you're my child, I didn't want to hurt you." I was crying. I didn't want anything to happen to her.

My mother didn't try to hurt me on purpose, but this was a consequence of the way she treated us. The mark was ugly; it took a week for my face to clear up.

Strict discipline was the way my mother thought was most appropriate for raising her children. I think in her mind she didn't want to hit us, but that is what she ended up doing, and I hated it. It got to the point where I was hating her. I didn't want to be like her. I was constantly thinking of the day when I would run away. I didn't want to be with her anymore.

Overall, then, it was only on occasion that she would get involved and play with us. I think her actions were influenced by what she was going through—the time of separation from my father. So, maybe her emotional feelings got in the way of spending time with her children and being happy with them. Possibly, her mind used to wonder "How am I going to do this? How am I going to raise these kids?" Maybe she was under a great deal of stress stemming from the divorce, and that made her behave the way she did.

In addition to her school responsibilities, Lourdes was involved in the Pentecostal church, which she started attending at an early age. Lourdes enjoyed this part of her life. The church brought her close to her aunt, the person she wanted to be like, and it was through church services and classes that Lourdes began to learn about the goodness inherent in every person. She learned, for instance, that, even when she was a very small child, she was held in high regard by Jesus Christ, and to Lourdes this was the ultimate gift. The Pentecostal church made Lourdes feel very special.

My life as a child also revolved around the Pentecostal church. This was also part of the family tradition. My grandmother was Pentecostal, and so was my mother. Of course, I was not going to be different. I was brought up as a churchgoing, religious person.

Like with school, I enjoyed going to church. I learned about God and about how to have faith and trust. The nurturing that I was receiving as a child helped me later on when hard times came. I don't recall opposing having to go to church at such an early age; in fact, I liked it. I enjoyed singing in church with other kids. Sometimes there was a program in church, and the kids were called up to sing; that was great because it gave us a chance to be recognized and to stand out. I also enjoyed attending the classes. It was a good feeling that has remained with me to this day.

Because of the church services and activities, I also was able to observe my aunt; she is one person I really like and respect. My aunt was our Sunday school teacher. I remember a song she taught us to sing: "Los niños son de Cristo, de Cristo, de Cristo. / Los niños son de Cristo, de Cristo El Señor" (The children are of Christ, of Christ, of Christ. / The children are of Christ, of Christ our Savior). Of course, what the song did for me was to make me realize that we were special. Here we were, this group of little kids who were being told that God was our Father; He, the Creator, saw us as being very special. We were His children, and He loved us. My aunt would make a point of emphasizing the importance of being good because, if we weren't, she would say, "He was going to cry." The most important thing that we were told was that we were very special, and I think that nothing can really equal the nurturing found in someone telling you: "You're special. Jesus loves you very much. You're very special." That has a major impact on a child. It certainly did to me.

My goal was to model myself after my aunt. I loved the way she cared for the children in Sunday school. She always tried teaching us about God—how he loves the little children and how special we were and how much we meant to him. She would tell us that God couldn't always be here with us and that's why he gave us a mother and father. And that we had to be good to them. I wanted to follow in her footsteps. I saw the way she was, so I thought I could be exactly like her. She is a very good Christian woman. Her ways are very loving. I love my mother very much, but I saw how my aunt was and said: "I want to be like her. I want to be a missionary and continue in church."

My aunt went out of her way to communicate with me, and I think in part it had to do with the fact that she had three sons and no daughter. So, I think she thought of me as the little girl she didn't have.

Divorce and its many complications came thundering into Lourdes's life when she was still very young. Confused and troubled over her parents' divorce when she was nine years old, Lourdes began to formulate ideas about men and women and their relationships. The trauma to her of her parents' divorce made Lourdes come to view marriage as a sacred and eternal act. She developed the idea that marriage should represent a lifetime association—that, no matter what the circumstances facing husband and wife, their major responsibility is to keep the marriage going. Lourdes was not about to repeat her parents' experience.

When I was nine my parents got a divorce. I didn't like the idea that they were separating. I didn't understand it. I didn't know what was happening, and then it got to the point where our mother was turning us against our father. Prior to their divorce they were separated for about a year or so, and I remember my father living in the basement of the church. My mother was always kind of cold toward him after that, and the coldness reflected on us. She would emphasize that this person was our father and that, no matter what happened between the two of them, we would have to love him— but she didn't say anything more than that.

Her behavior was very hard for us because we love our father dearly. And she was really bitter, but we couldn't understand why; after all, we never saw our father doing anything wrong. He was always protecting us. There were times when my mother would come and try to hit us with her belt, and he would get in the way and sometimes end up getting whipped himself because he would get in front of us. She was always fighting with him because of that. To this day I cannot remember my father lifting a hand to hit any of us. Maybe he hit my brother—I don't remember. But I do remember that he wasn't mean.

The reason they got a divorce is something that was never clear enough for me to understand. My mother thinks it was because they didn't have a long courtship and there wasn't much love. She just got married because that was a way of her escaping from my grandfather and grandmother. I think when they sent her to Chicago it was with the understanding that, after a certain period of time, she would have to return. So, she decided to get married instead. The idea was that, if she was married, she didn't have to return to Puerto Rico and live with them.

So, when they got married there wasn't that moment of magic. No, I don't believe they ever experienced that special moment that says: "Oh, this is the love of my life. I will love this person to death do us part." I don't really think their love was like that.

They were married for almost ten years. My mother realized long before the divorce that there wasn't much love. She decided to stick to it because of us. We were small, and she wanted us to have some understanding of what was going on. When they finally divorced I still didn't understand. She said that, right after she had my sister, she didn't love my father anymore. All her feelings for him disappeared. She tried to work things out, but there was something about him that prevented her from developing feelings of love for him. The only thing I can gather from the different times that we would eavesdrop was that she liked my father because he was a good provider, but she didn't find him fit to be her husband because she couldn't love him anymore.

Of course, after the divorce we remained living with my mother. And then at one point during the separation my father came and told us, "If you guys go to court, they are going to make you choose where you would stay." So, the two of them had us in this situation of confusion. I wish they knew how difficult it was for us. We couldn't have made a choice. They were people that we loved. We used to cry at night that we would never have to go to court and make this difficult choice.

I think that because of that experience at my early age is why I engraved in my mind that, no matter what, I was going to make my marriage work. The more I think about it, I think a lot of things from that experience led to my circumstances. I was so firm to not let that happen to me. My marriage was going to work because it was not going to be like my mother's.

My mother was suffering as well, but then it got to the point that she stopped going to church. She started going out and we didn't like that. We didn't see anything bad happening, but she was going out to dances. We were kids, but we knew what happens at dances. Then phone calls started coming in the middle of the night. We would see her sneaking around too.

It's not that my mother was a loose woman. It wasn't that. I guess she was trying to say that she wasn't going to settle down with the first man that came around. I think that's what was in her mind, and I also think she found out who she really loved because she's been married to my stepfather for seventeen years.

This was another moment in our lives which I didn't care for. I was beginning to be a young lady, and I didn't like the way men that came over to see her looked at me and my sister. Though we never told this to my mother, I didn't like them. They were—I don't want to say perverts, but they were men that acted fresh. They tried getting close to me and my sister. They liked to touch a lot. And, although they never went any further than that, I didn't like any other man [besides my father] putting his arm around me and kissing me on the cheek and saying, "Oh, you're such a pretty girl." I didn't like that. I didn't think they were doing these things in an innocent way.

My relationship with my stepfather has always been very good. At first he made the point of winning us over. I think even before he won my mother over he had won us. When he visited he would always bring candy and talk to us in a very positive way. He went out of his way to tell us that he wasn't taking over, that he just wanted to be our friend. I guess that's why we got along with him so well—he made it clear that he wasn't there to be our father. At that age of ten or twelve some stepfathers make the kids call them Dad. Well, it wasn't like that with our stepfather. I remember my father and him meeting and even going out to baseball games together and having an open relationship because he wanted to let my father know that he wasn't taking his place.

During her childhood and adolescence school and church occupied most of Lourdes's waking hours, yet her mother's prohibitive discipline made her life uncomfortable. She felt that her life lacked essential outlets for releasing some of the energy she naturally had as a teenager.

It is true that most, if not all, families impose some sort of stress on family members, including the children. A family is a complex system, and each of its members has certain limitations, flaws, and behaviors that may help or hinder the family's circumstances. A particular family value or behavior may become insupportable over time and provoke some members to oppose it; even if these actions are risky, they at least represent a change. Of course, in some families these stresses are more severe than in others.

Because many of her friends inquired about the kind of life she was leading, Lourdes assumed hers was an unusual family situation. It was her psychological distress that prompted Lourdes to challenge the values of her own family. She found herself opposing the dominant values that for so long had controlled her life and began to believe that her personal development and friendships should take precedence over achievement at school—or, at the very least, the two should go hand in hand.

The seclusion and isolation from other kids in school and in the neighborhood was difficult to endure. So, when I met my boyfriend, when I was in eighth grade and he was in high school, we decided to get married shortly after. It was less than a year later that we got married. It probably wouldn't have happened that way had I been allowed to do and try some of the things that other kids were doing. My mother did not give me the opportunity to see other guys. I didn't have other choices. There was this other guy that I liked, but he ended up going to Puerto Rico, so, that ended that. Besides, that was puppy love. So, it was that my mother was simply too overprotective. I was suffocating under her rules. And with young children, if you say no, they are going to do the opposite sometimes just to oppose you. I was one of those who decided to do things differently. Of course, I paid and to some extent continue to pay for the consequences. If I were to live my life over again, however, I would change very little.

Everything changed when I turned fifteen. I was already in high school, and that's when I started getting closer and falling more in love with my boyfriend. All the pressure from my friends about becoming one of them finally did it. They would tell me to stop being like I was and to fit in. Conditions were overwhelming me. I was young and confused. What my friends were saying took over me in the sense that I wanted to show them that I was what they wanted. I wanted to show them that I could be with them, that I was not afraid of cutting classes.

This is not what I wanted to do. I didn't like doing these things, but I wanted to be liked. Though I should've stood my ground, when it came to the point that they were telling me that he liked me I saw that, in order for him to see that I really liked him, I needed to show him that I wasn't a homey girl. I had to let him know that I went out and that I wasn't shy, because that's what he was being told about me.

One of the first things I did was to stop attending church. I felt bad about it at the time, but I really didn't give it much thought. I wanted to do my own thing, and I thought I was making the right decisions. My friends in church were sad to see me go. My mother was against it because I was the only one in the family who was still going. She raised us in the church, and she felt that's the best way to be. But it was hard for her to tell me, though she was my mother, "You go to church, and you dress this way." She just wasn't doing it; my sister wasn't doing it—so why should I? I felt that religion—or, for that matter, anything else—can't be imposed by someone that isn't practicing what she is preaching.

It was crazy. I was enjoying going out. I was becoming involved with the people my mother did not like or want me to be with. Here I was—the same girl who was not permitted to do anything—doing it all.

In my days at church, I was a very conservative girl. When I stopped attending I started wearing makeup, pants, and short dresses. It was like I was letting people see that here I was. This was who I was. It wasn't like I was wild, but I wanted to go out to parties and dances and have a nice time. I just wanted to do the things that I had not been permitted to do for most of my life.

I even started a little group of girls. Yes, it was weird. I was establishing a girls' gang. That's what introduced me to gang activity. At first I thought it was just a group of people hanging out. That view changed when I got involved in one fight. One time, coming out of high school, there was this girl who came looking for me. She said that she heard I was organizing these girls, and she wanted to fight me because I wasn't supposed to be doing that in her neighborhood. I decided not to fight her. I realized very quickly that this girl could easily kill me—I walked away. At other times I got really scared. We were carrying knives. We thought we were really bad.

After these experiences I learned that this wasn't for me. I didn't like it very much. So, I decided to quit the gang. One girl in the gang did not like me because she liked my boyfriend, who was a leader, and when I decided to leave the gang she said that I couldn't just leave. She tried to make a case about not allowing members to just walk out of the gang. She said that I needed to be violated out [beaten up], and I told them that I was going to leave without having them all hit me. I realized after three months of gang stuff that it wasn't for me.

My involvement with the gang was a way of showing my boyfriend that I was down, that I was not afraid to be part of the street scene. Being down is a practice many young people in our neighborhood carry out. Both males and females must demonstrate their willingness to take risks. Young people gain respect by showing that they are down: that they are not afraid, that they support a particular gang. This is one of the better-known rules of the streets.

All along I recognized that what I was doing was not positive or gracious, but it felt great. I was going out with my boyfriend when all the other girls wanted to go out with him, and they couldn't. I thought I found my catch.

Like her decision to organize and form a girls' gang, Lourdes made a decision to get married almost spontaneously. At the age of fifteen, while in her first year of high school—and in opposition to the views of many around her—Lourdes made what has become the biggest decision of her life.

When we were married I was very young. I was going through many difficult and confusing times. I was very naive. I thought love could conquer and remedy everything. Marriage was a way out of my troubles. Obviously, it didn't turn out like that.

I can almost say that our marriage was something that just happened. One day when I was going out with him he came to pick me up, and I was feeling frustrated because my mother didn't like him. If I went to the show with him to see a movie, I had to take my brother or sister. I thought that I couldn't do the things I wanted to do. I wasn't planning to do anything bad. I just wanted to go out and walk in the park like I saw other girls doing—things like that. But I couldn't. In fact, my mother selected days when he could come over to see me. I think she allowed him to visit me on Wednesdays and Fridays. For the visits he was required by my mother to be nicely dressed. He would come upstairs to our apartment, and we would sit in the living room and watch TV. On days when the weather was nice we would sit in front of our building and talk. My mother was always around in the house making sure I didn't go anywhere. My boyfriend never said much about these restrictions, but I think he felt somewhat offended because he is not the person that other people make him out to be. He felt that there was no reason for my mother to fear him the way she did. I used to ask my mother, "Why do you do this to me?" But I also knew that, if I wanted to see him, this was the only way it was going to be possible.

Another very important thing happened that has to do with our decision to get married. We lived about two blocks away from one another. As I soon as I started getting more attached to him, my mother decided that it was time for us to move. And we moved. We went to live in a different neighborhood. It wasn't like moving to another country; it wasn't very far. My mother was just trying to get me away from him. It didn't work. In fact, this action drew us closer because I resented her more. In addition, he came to school for me, and I ended up going home much later because he had a car, and it was no problem since he could drive me home. All this time I was thinking, "You don't understand how I feel about this person."

The next thing she did was to threaten me with the idea of sending me to Puerto Rico to stay with my grandmother. I told my boyfriend, "Listen, if she sends me to Puerto Rico, I'm going to write you, tell you where I am so you can send for me." So, she knew real quickly that I would have contacted my boyfriend, and he would have sent for me. The idea flew out of the window. She understood better than to send me away to Puerto Rico. The problem was that there wasn't much communication.

So, this one particular day he came to visit me, and we went downstairs to talk. He asked me what was wrong, and I said: "I'm so mad. I just want to get married." I wasn't asking him to marry me; I was just making a statement. I think that he understood what I said differently and asked me, "Do you want to get married?" Like a month later he came over and brought a ring. We got engaged and were married in December that same year. It all happened so fast.

When my husband and I got married it was with a lot of opposition, from both my family and somewhat his family. My mother wanted me to continue school; she was afraid I'd drop out and leave my studies behind. She was afraid I wasn't going to do all the things I wanted to.

I can understand now. I was her fifteen-year-old daughter, her first daughter, and she wanted the best for me. And I had fallen in love with someone who, by society's standards, is no good. This is the way she thought about what was happening to me. I, on the other hand, didn't see my husband as being bad, even though I was aware of what he did. I imagined that he would grow out of his gang involvement. But she didn't see it that way. She felt I was going into a marriage where I would be abused and I would be placed in a basement with nothing. This was the picture she had developed in her mind about our married life.

This was the only time I ever really spoke out because I defended my husband to the very end. I told her that things were not going to turn out the way she was thinking—that he wasn't like that, that he was good, that she shouldn't think that. I also told her not to listen to other people because she always told us not to listen to other people's opinions, that people don't pay your rent, and here she was listening to what people were saying about him. I told her: "You don't know him. You wouldn't hit me for what I'm doing, but you still do slap me down by saying that I'm too young and that I think I know it all. You don't understand—I love him."

The problem was that my mother didn't care for him because of what people were telling her. People told my mother only negative images of my boyfriend. I thought she was entitled to hear the positive things as well; after all, everyone has only negative images of my boyfriend. I thought she was entitled to hear the positive things as well; after all, everyone has a good and bad side. When I was going out with my husband he was even presented to my mother as a junkie. He was not a junkie—this was not his style. He used drugs, but he was never a junkie. I thought that this was a young life that people were destroying by saying all those negative things. He was being made into this hopeless human being, and I couldn't accept that.

My father took a somewhat different attitude toward my marriage. He wasn't living with us because by this time he was married to someone else. He didn't see what was going on. He just wanted to be a good father. He told me that, if that was what I wanted, he would go along with it because he didn't want to go against me. So, the only thing I remember is that my father promised to buy me a car. I think he was trying to bribe me. I suppose my father was trying to exchange a car for my decision not to marry. That didn't work either. I didn't want a car. I wanted to get married. So, he didn't give me a hard time.

My mother got mad at my father because he decided to approve of my decision. She was upset because he didn't set his foot down and say, "No, this is it." She wanted my father to come out and beat on my husband and say to him, "Leave my daughter alone." Of course, my father didn't do that. Though I wanted my father to give me away at the wedding, that was something he couldn't face. My father went to the reception, but, because he felt so heart-broken, my stepfather was the one who gave me away. Even my brother stayed in the bedroom during the ceremony. They all felt I was making this huge mistake, and they were partly right. But I wanted them to understand that it was my mistake that I was going to make. I wanted them to let me deal with it. I didn't see it their way; I was going to prove everybody wrong.

I really believe that they wanted the best for me, and they had good intentions at heart. But the way they went about it was wrong. They should have sat me down and said: "If you want to date this guy, fine, but make yourself available to other people because that's permissible. Don't rush into anything." Instead, they would tell me things like, "This is a gang member, a drug dealer, that you're get-ting yourself involved with." They did everything the total opposite way. And the more you tell a young person not to do something, the quicker that person is going to do it.

There was also one teacher in school who was opposed to my marriage. He was totally against it because he knew my husband. I was a freshman, and my husband was a junior, and for three years he had been a troublemaker at the school. On the other hand, here I was, going to all of my classes. I was far from being a trouble-maker. I joined the ROTC [Reserve Officers' Training Corps] be-cause I didn't want to take swimming because I didn't want to put on a bathing suit—I was still very conservative. Then all of a sudden I decided that this was the guy I wanted to marry. For many people it was like night and day. And I remember this particular teacher—he told me: "Lourdes, you're making a big mistake. I give you one year at most." I was sick of these people telling me what my life was going to be like. I knew there would be problems, but I was sure that I would make it.

Finally, I told my mother that I was going to get married whether she liked it or not. She wasn't going to stop me. I was determined to run away if that was what it took. I didn't want to do that because I wanted to have a wedding. Having a wedding for me was very important. I wanted to be the first in our immediate family to do so. Besides, people used to think that all Puerto Rican girls simply eloped, that they were not the marrying type. I set out to dispel that myth.

I told my mother in October that we were going to get married. We scheduled the wedding for June 1977, when I turned sixteen. But my mother said, "If you want to get married, you'll have to do it by December." She gave us two months to plan the wedding. She figured that it could not be done in such a short period of time. I went with my husband and got an apartment, bought some furniture, and got ready for the big day.

What is interesting is that the wedding was basically planned by my family; my mother did everything. I came in one night, and my sister told me to come to the room and see what was there waiting for me. I entered the room to find boxes of sheets and pots and dishes and utensils. My mother had bought everything for the house. But what is just as interesting is that she never gave them to me. My mother never came and said, "Lourdes, this is for you." There was nothing coming out of her mouth. She never even told me about the nightgown she bought me for my honeymoon. She would just buy these things and leave them for me. She was hurt, yet she went out of her way to buy me whatever I needed.

I felt good because I thought it showed a way of concern. I thought that this was her way of wanting me to have the best. But I missed the part of her asking me, "Lourdes, do you like what I bought you?" I remember she took me out to lunch a week before the wedding because we needed to talk. We went out and ate, but we never talked. She couldn't bring herself to talk about anything in depth about relationships or anything.

Because the church where I wanted to have the wedding was under repairs, we had the reception at his aunt's house. It was a small wedding. I wanted it to be family. Also, I didn't want his [my husband's] friends there, breaking it up. I didn't want my mother to say: "Look, I knew I was right. Look at all these gang members here." It was not that I didn't like them—we had grown very close. I didn't want to give my family the upper hand of talking and saying "I told you so." So, the wedding was very private, with our families there and very few friends.

2

Marriage to a Gang Member

Marriage was the sum total of the ultimate love and closeness Lourdes felt for and wanted to share with her husband for life. It symbolized the supreme meaning embodied in the cultural expression "Because of the way I feel for you, I want us to spend the rest of our lives together."

At the same time marriage also represented a direct way for Lourdes to wrest freedom from her mother and gain control over her life and mind; for Lourdes it meant personal liberation and empowerment. Marriage justified Lourdes's desire to distance herself from a home environment that she felt was extraordinarily repressive, and she believed that marriage would provide her with the room to run her life according to her own decisions and not her mother's. In this way Lourdes was essentially repeating her mother's action of a generation before.

There are many reasons why I decided to get married at such an early age. I knew that I had found the person who I wanted to spend the rest of my life with. At the time I was convinced that I had found the person that only comes into your life once. Of course, when he showed up into my life I knew it was him. So, what do people do in these situations? They go with their heart and feelings and choose what is most natural. For me the natural thing to do was to marry my husband.

I also wanted to live my own life. I wanted my independence. Once I was married I knew that I would be in my house setting the rules. I was going to have responsibility for a husband and not for a mother. I was the one who was going to make the decisions.

It is interesting that my reasons for getting married are pretty much the same as my mother's. Through marriage she had gained sufficient freedom and space for making her own decisions. She got married so she would not have to go back to Puerto Rico where her parents had brought her up pretty much the same way she had done with me. This is essentially why I got married. Yet she could not understand why I decided to do what I did.

I tried to make my mother see that, if I was making a mistake, it was going to be my mistake. Though it was going to hurt her, because I was her daughter, I wanted her to grant me the opportunity to make my own decision. If my marriage did not work out and failed, well, it failed, but I didn't want her to impose and to say, "You're not going do this." I felt like I could handle the situation.

It wasn't until my mother called my grandmother [her mother] in Puerto Rico and talked to her that my mother finally agreed to go along with my plans. My grandmother told her to let me do what I was asking; otherwise, I could decide to run away. My grandmother thought that to elope would bring shame to the family. My grandmother told my mother that, if things didn't work out, it would be something we would have to fix later as a family. And that's when my mother finally decided to okay the marriage.

The first couple of months of marriage for Lourdes were filled with honey-moon romance and caring. Although she was placed in a subordinate posi-

tion—a place all too familiar to Puerto Rican women at the time—Lourdes believed she had found a way of life more gratifying and pleasant than the one she was leaving behind. From all appearances the marriage was working out.

Lourdes's husband's involvement in the gang was too strong, however, for marriage to pull him away from the streets and into the conventional husband role she had assumed he would fall into. Lourdes's hopes that she could change her husband were met by the magnetic pull of the youth, street gang. Similar to the gender-split socialization process of Puerto Rican youngsters—wherein the life of boys exists in the streets, while girls are relegated to in-house activities—the gang requires its members to spend a great deal of time on the street corner. Being a leader of his gang, the amount of time that Lourdes's husband was away from her and their house was even greater.

Thus, physical separation constituted a leading feature of Lourdes's marriage. Over time Lourdes came to understand and adjust to the condition of having to share her husband with the streets of the city.

When we first got married everything was like a fairy tale. It was really sweet. I enjoyed myself a lot. I was young. I was only fifteen, and here I was—in this house that was mine. The furniture was mine; everything was mine. My husband was working and going to school, while I was just attending school. Although the days became fairly routine, they were filled with much fun. After I got home from school I would just wait for him. I would then cook. After dinner he would go out, and I stayed home and watched television. We would spend a lot of time together. Sometimes we would go and visit my family or his. Instead of coming home to tell my mother what I had done in school, I was coming home to be with my husband. I was in control. It was all mine.

I remember our first apartment. It was like a doll house. It was small but just right for two persons. It was really cute. Since my husband was working, he saved some money and asked one of his uncles to co-sign so we could buy furniture. So, we furnished the apartment with all new things. On top of that we had a puppy, which, unfortunately, we had to get rid of because he would cry all the time. One of my husband's younger brothers got us the puppy as a wedding gift. We were very sad when we realized that we could not keep the puppy because he added to the character of the family. To me everything looked very nice.

The apartment was on the first floor of a single-family house, whose attic had been expanded into a flat by the owners so they could live there. The owners were two little, old people. They were white and truly wonderful. Their children had grown up and had gone off on their own. They did not have grandchildren. As a result, they went on to love us very much because we represented for them the grandchildren they did not have. And it was like having their grandchildren there with them all the time. When they discovered that I was pregnant they became really excited. They were looking forward to seeing my first child; they were going to be outstanding grandparents.

These were very good times for me. I felt so lucky. As far as I could see, everything was going to be wonderful.

I wanted my husband to be just like a traditional husband and father. I wanted him to be with me and not with his friends. I used to think that the two of us would go to church together. My goal was to have a family life, to be working, to be comfortable. That was what the American Dream was based on. I was going to pursue this dream. I didn't think about his background as a gang leader or his gang activities. I thought I would change all of that. In my mind I was convinced that his relationship with the streets and his friends, everything he did before, would be forgotten once we were married.

I never spoke to him about my dreams and ideas. I thought that he saw and wanted pretty much the same things as I did. So, I didn't think it was necessary to share with him these things. Besides, when you're dating and telling your future husband about your ideas and plans he is going to support them. He will say yes to anything you say and ask. He, in turn, will promise you the stars.

Things didn't happen exactly how I had expected. At my age I couldn't have realized that you can't just change overnight the life a person has lived for umpteen years. I was young and hopeful. I believed that there was nothing that I couldn't change, including my husband. I used to think that, after a little time with me, he would see things my way. Instead, after the fourth month of marriage everything went up in a puff of smoke. My husband was heavily involved in his gang, and the gang mattered a great deal to him.

At that time in my life I knew little about gangs. When I was in eighth grade my opinion about gangs was that they just did bad things. I used to think of gang members as robbing and stealing from people as well as beating up on them. It was really a negative perception. At that time my idea about the gangs was the same as my mother's: gangs are bad because they do bad things.

If I knew one thing for sure, it was that I didn't like gangs. I didn't like the idea of the gang, which is different than saying "I don't like its members." Some of the guys were alright, but it was the idea of functioning as a gang and doing the kinds of things they were carrying out in the neighborhood. After you meet the guys and learn about them as individuals you can't help but like them.

Before we got married, even before we started going out, I had heard some people in the neighborhood define my husband as the kind of leader who had this enormous control over some other guys. I used to think: "Who does he think he is? How could someone at the age of seventeen be so powerful, so controlling?" I thought he was just a spoiled kid. So, the first time I saw him I hated him because I knew what he was up to. I remember going up to him and telling him "You think you're so bad." He didn't say anything. He smiled and didn't take what I said in a bad way.

Instead, he went and told one of his friends that I was going to marry him because I was stubborn.

I was very surprised by the way he responded when I confronted him. I was expecting him to be very rude, to be nasty and to say something bad, because that's how he was portrayed to be. But he didn't. I guess it's true that you can't judge a book by its cover; you need to find out how the person really is before you can start passing judgment. From that moment on I started looking at him differently. As funny as it may seem, I began thinking that he couldn't be all that bad. I was left with the impression of him having a good side.

Yet my husband was one of the gang members. I knew that he was involved in the gang and that opposing gangs in the neighborhood were fighting each other. And, although we were having a wonderful time together, life was difficult. The life of the wife of a gang member is a horrible life. Just recently I was talking to a neighbor who has a daughter who is falling for a young man involved in a gang. The neighbor was telling me that her daughter was upset at her boyfriend because he was invited to go to the lake and decided not to primarily because he was anticipating some kind of problem to occur there. The girl was all upset because she thought that it was that he just didn't want to take her. I said to the mother that, if her daughter likes this guy and chooses to have a future with him, their lives are going to be limited insofar as which places they are going to be able to go. She looked at me and asked me what I meant, and I told her that my life was limited. I informed her that it got to the point that I would just sit at home because we couldn't go to public places because of fear that someone would recognize him and start trouble. I don't remember us saying "Let's go dancing, or to the movie, or let's take a stroll in the park." I told her that we couldn't do those things and that I missed doing every one of them. Today my husband realizes that those are some of the things that we were deprived of because of his gang involvement.

I was also telling my neighbor that I lived in constant fear, always thinking that something bad was going to happen to him. If the phone rang in the middle of the night, the first thing I would think was, "Oh, no, he was shot." It was a constant battle of nerves not knowing what could happen every night. There were times when we were in the car going somewhere, and when we came to a red light he would stop very far from the cars in front. He would also look from side to side. I was so annoyed by that. I couldn't understand it. I would argue with him, and he would just say that he needed to be on guard.

Another thing was that my husband didn't talk much about what he was doing. Even to this day he remains a private person when it comes to gang activities. It's funny because his friends sometimes talk and say things without realizing that I don't have any previous knowledge of what they're talking about. They think that just because I'm his wife I automatically know. So, I pretend to know. I listen carefully. Then I would come and tell my husband, "Well, I didn't know that this or that had happened." And he would say, "How did you learn about that?" As much as he tries to shield me or protect me, sooner or later I find out. But at the moment when things were happening I knew so little.

So, I came to the decision that the best way for me to deal with this code of silence was not to get involved. Every time I asked him about something that I learned had happened he would just say: "Nothing happened. Don't worry about it." So, I said, "Well, forget it." I began to stay home more. If I was to remain sane, then the less I knew about what he was doing, the better it was.

I saw other wives and girlfriends of gang members follow their husband or boyfriend to the corner to tell him, "Let's go home," or whatever. I also saw the rejection they felt when they were told to go home themselves and not to bother. I observed this, and I thought, "He's never going to have the opportunity to tell me in front of other people to go home. I'm not going to let him embarrass me in public." So, I decided not to get involved. There was nothing that I could do. What was the use? Why get involved?

I think that other wives were insecure about their husbands. They used to worry that they would be spending time with other women. I used to think that whatever he did [with other women] would always amount to a great loss. He knew what he had at home.

What I was doing at that time appears passive: I wasn't getting involved, and I was allowing my husband do whatever he wanted. That has something to do with the way I was brought up. I was more of a homebound person. I wasn't one to go out late and stay out dancing all night. So, I made home my place to be. At home I was in control. I had the upper hand at home. The streets belonged to him, but our house was mine. It represented the only solid ground that I had to stand on. I was in charge there. My husband recognized and accepted that. He always respected what I said about what was permissible in our home.

Of course, although I decided not to go after him when he was out on the streets, I worried a great deal. To this day I continue to worry, and I always think the same thing, "Oh, God, what's going to happen?" And when things do happen the first recourse that I have is to pray. But, still, I think and worry about what's going on. He doesn't want me to know what he's doing or did because he doesn't want me to worry about something that I can't do anything about.

There is a popular saying among gang members that gang participation leads to only two possible outcomes: death or imprisonment. Within the context of gang rivalry and conflict which existed in el barrio *during this period, the mid-1970s to early 1980s, it is not surprising that such a view was common among those in gangs and those outside them. It is estimated that over twenty major gangs and their many affiliates were at war to control drug distribution in Lourdes's community in the late 1970s and early 1980s, and their activities were well known to the entire community.*

In the case of Lourdes's husband, anoher man's death put him in prison. Having been accused of shooting a rival gang member, he was sent to prison shortly after his marriage to Lourdes began—exactly four months later.

Because I knew of what he was doing, I wasn't so surprised when he got locked up. It seemed that I was expecting something like that to happen. When he was arrested for the first time I was with him. It had to do with a big shoot-out involving two rival gangs. It happened right in front of his parents' house. My husband belonged to one of the gangs. One guy from a rival gang that was at war with my husband's was killed. Because my husband was known to be a leader, the members of the other gang accused him, when, in fact, he was home with me. We were newlyweds.

My husband already had several [arrest] cases for drug dealing and for standing on the corner [loitering], so these guys went to the police station and looked through the mug shots until they came across a picture of my husband and one of his brother. It was truly amazing. Here we had a situation of members of one gang accusing others from a rival gang. What is even more entertaining is that the police bought the story. Or, better yet, this is the story the police were after. The police wanted someone, regardless of the person's identity, to finger my husband and to be willing to present testimony in court against him.

I wasn't totally naive about my husband's involvement with the gang and his arrest record. I remember learning about one early arrest one time when his mother asked me to serve as a translator at the police station. I didn't understand why he was arrested. His mother simply told me not to worry, that it was nothing. She told me that the police just caught him on the corner. I guess I believed her, because the guys were not allowed to hang out. When they were together standing on the corner and the police arrested them, they were charged with loitering. It was claimed that hanging out entailed engaging in gang activity, which included drug dealing and harassing people who came by.

For my husband the answer for his arrests was always the same: "It wasn't me. I was at the wrong place at the wrong time. Everything is going to be okay." He never gave me a direct answer. After a few years it became a part of life.

There is no denying that my husband knew what was happening. In the late 1970s the neighborhood was the site of this little war. Opposing gangs were shooting at one another. There was money to be made through the sale of drugs, and different gangs were competing with one another to control the market. It seemed like every day a gang member was killed or injured from gang fights.

My husband was one of those who was arrested and eventually charged for one such killing. Although he wasn't involved in the shooting, he ended up serving. At first his brother was the only one arrested, an action I couldn't understand, since pictures of both my husband and his brother had been identified. I have always wondered why my husband wasn't locked up along with his brother. Of course, he would get arrested at a later date; it happened when we went to court for his brother's preliminary hearings. One witness pointed to where my husband and I were sitting and said that my husband had been involved in the shooting. The police, who were serving as courtroom guards, were ordered to come to where we were to arrest him. I was four months' pregnant at the time, and in the course of the police trying to arrest him they hit me. The force of the push made me hit a wall; my whole back rammed into the wall, because they really wanted to get him. They took him and left me there. The whole family was hysterical.

Finally, the county sheriffs came to give me first aid, though I wasn't sure this is what they really intended to do. They took me to an office downstairs from the courtroom and gave me water and first aid. The public defender, who was assigned to handle my brother-in-law's case, tried to reassure me that everything was going to be okay, that he was going to take me to the police station where we could talk. He drove me to the police station.

I didn't know at this time what was happening. I had no idea what my husband was being arrested for. A state's attorney started questioning me. I was afraid to tell him anything because I hadn't spoken to my husband. The state's attorney wanted to question me before I had a chance to talk to my husband; apparently, he was hoping that we would not get our stories straight. He asked me about my whereabouts at the time of the shooting, whether I was with my husband or not. I responded by asking him, "What are you talking about?" I honestly did not know what they were talking about. I didn't even know what was happening to begin with, and all of a sudden here is this man asking me: "Where were you on such and such a date? What was the time? What did you eat that day?" And every time he asked me a question he would also say, "This is voluntary: you don't have to answer." So, I figured, "If I don't have to answer you, then leave me alone." Finally, after seeing that I would not talk they took me to a little room where they were holding my husband.

To this day I still remember vividly the witness who identified my husband in the courtroom. I'll never forget him. I was so angry. He pointed out my husband and just smirked at me. When he did this I couldn't believe what I was witnessing. He knew he was not telling the truth. I was pregnant. It is quite apparent that he didn't care about the suffering that we were all going to go through. I developed an enormous amount of hate then. Now I have forgiven it all. They were all so young. They were ignorant. They didn't care about wives, mothers, sisters. The only things they believed in were the gang and getting even. That was their priorities. Even now their philosophy is "death before dishonor."

The next day, after this incident had happened in the court-room, I had a miscarriage, due to the severe bruises I suffered from the way the police had decided to handle the situation. I did not understand that I had a miscarriage. I could not understand that it could be happening to me. I thought that I had everything, and all of a sudden everything was being taken away from me, including my baby. When I had the miscarriage my husband wasn't there, because he had been incarcerated. And here I was losing our first child. It was like the floor was being ripped from under me, and I could not understand most of what was happening.

Assured by doctors that she would lead a normal life, Lourdes looked for-ward to having and raising her own children. During the time that her husband was not in prison, they tried to become parents. There was nothing that Lourdes wanted more than to become pregnant, but that was not to be.

Lourdes became angry and frustrated, deciding finally to take the police department to court for its improper treatment, which, she believes, caused her not to be able to have children.

I was told by the doctor that I was fine and I could have children in the future. I went through a series of tests, including fertility medi-cation, but I was not able to get pregnant again. The doctors could not understand why I could not conceive. A woman doctor told me that she thought that the problem was that, since I wanted to have a baby so much, it probably was keeping me from achieving it. She told me to relax and not to think about it, but that did not work either.

I felt terrible not being able to have children. I love children. To me children are the ones who make the home. Children represent the best gift God gave to women. It is the woman who feels the heartbeats of the baby. She feels all the movements. As much as she tries to relay those sentiments to the husband, he can never feel what she does. I think that's very special.

Later I sued the police department, and we settled out of court. That was another major ordeal I faced. Every attorney I contacted refused to take my case because suppossedly the baby was at the stage of a fetus. What they were saying was that it was only four months, and I could have lost it anyway because I was so young. I was not even sixteen years old yet, but I had seen so much abuse. I wasn't going to put up with that anymore. Here I was, something very terrible had happened to me—a life was taken from me—and I was supposed to remain quiet. That's the impression I got from the attorneys I contacted. They were making the case look like I was trying to prevent the arrest of my husband. And I said, "No, I'm not going to stay quiet." I was going to let them see and hear that I had a voice.

I finally found an attorney who agreed that the whole thing was unjust. I almost gave up on the case because it took so long. The case went on year after year, and I just didn't care how long it took. I wasn't going after the police department's money. I just wanted justice to be served. It was quite clear that no amount of money was going to bring my child back. It was just that I wanted to let them know they were wrong in what they did. Because of that experience, I learned that we can't just stay quiet and that those kinds of incidents have happened for too long in our community, where people allow police brutality to exist because of fear. The police are supposed to help us, and they have to acknowledge when they are doing something wrong. They are not above the law.

Over the years I have witnessed how aggressive the police tend to be when dealing with the guys from the neighborhood because they are not supposed to stand on the corner. I feel that to some extent the police have the right to do what they do, but they shouldn't handcuff the guys just for standing. And then after they're handcuffed, why must they hit them over the head with the billy clubs or with the guns? Why should they tear off their shirts? Sometimes the police come walking in the neighborhood and, for no reason, slap some guy on the head. I remember witnessing cases when the police would drive into the neighborhood, pick up one of the guys, and take him to the turf of an opposition gang and yell out the name of his gang.

I don't believe they have the right to do those things. The cops knew that these cases were hard to prove, that there was no way anyone was going to believe a gang member. It wasn't until people from the community started filing complaints that I started seeing a little change here and there. As you know, people are now having to take pictures and use videotapes in order to have a legitimate case against police brutality. But that kind of stuff has been going on in our community for a long time.

Lourdes's husband's incarceration produced an irreparable rupture in Lourdes's life.

Lourdes had to leave her dollhouse apartment to go live with her mother. Her family, including her husband, could not accept the idea of a young Puerto Rican woman living alone. Thus, Lourdes was reunited with her mother, with whom she began to communicate better.

Lourdes was rejoined by her husband six months later. He returned, how-ever, more filled with hate toward members of opposition gangs. He felt strongly that he had been treated unfairly, and the time had come for retalia-tion. He was determined to go all out to avenge himself. For the first time Lourdes understood that her husband's behavior was not going to change. She recognized that, regardless what she did or said, her husband was going to be involved in a gang and that the gang was his main priority in life.

When my husband was incarcerated for those false charges I had to leave my own home, my own apartment. I went to live with my mother. Actually, I didn't want to leave, but my mother didn't see any reason why I needed to be alone and paying rent. My husband also encouraged her to try to convince me to go with her. And I did. We decided to store the furniture in the basement of my aunt's house.

Though my husband was out in six months, that was my first experience with serious grief. I was really ignorant about what was prison or jail life or anything like it. As time passed, I began to learn about the fights that went on inside and the rapes of some guys. In essence, I learned about all the abuse that takes place in jail. For visitors of inmates there were the searches. I was being subjected to having someone feel me all over to see if I was bringing some kind of contraband. Even with female officers women visitors have to submit themselves to all of these things that are very private to them. This was all new to me. I was shocked. But, like other women, I had to agree to the searches and other harassments in order to see the person on the other side.

When I went to visit him I had to carry my marriage license in order to prove that we were married, because I was still fifteen years old, and I was considered a minor. At times I would make the visits with my mother so they would believe that I was a wife. Think about it for a minute—my mother served as justification for my marital status. This was a devastating experience for me. Here I was, married, and yet I could only see my husband on terms established by someone else. While I was a married woman, people were still seeing me as a kid. I felt I was being given the runaround, that I was being treated more unfairly than others. I didn't like that. But now I understand that they wanted to be careful for their safety.

When I came to live with my mother it was easy to see the hurt she was feeling. I could tell that she knew and could feel the pain I was suffering. I also could tell that she knew that there was very little she could do to comfort me. If there is one thing for sure, it is that she remembered warning me about all of this, though even to this day she has never said, "I told you so." I'm very grateful and thankful for that.

On many occasions I just wanted her to hold me, but she wouldn't. I guess she didn't know what to say or what to do. So, I would just remain quite and not say anything either. I never told her how I felt.

There were so many times when I just wanted to run to her and say, "Mom, it hurts so much." But I didn't want her to hurt any more than I was. So, I just kept it inside. Then there were other times when I would come home from work and tell her how much I was missing my husband. But I always played that strong role— that everything was going to be just fine. I would not even allow her to see me cry.

Latino people are very emotional. They cry at the drop of a hat. I am like that for sure. But around my mother I disciplined myself so I would not cry or break down. I think I was trying to protect her feelings. I didn't let her see me hurt or see me cry.

It wasn't easy coming back to live with my mother, and it was not that she wasn't understanding or caring. I feel that she was extremely concerned with my situation. She showed me how much she cared. Her understanding of my situation could be witnessed from her decision not to make any comments about it. She didn't want to hurt me; she knew that anything anyone said at that time was going to make me feel more pain and sorrow. Her silence was, in a way, her form of protecting her daughter, who was very much in grief.

With the marriage my mother's attitude changed. She was totally different. She looked at me differently. I was a woman and not a little girl anymore. She was loving. Maybe she thought we had more in common now.

So, it wasn't my mother. My sister was the one who added aggravation to my condition. I have always loved my sister dearly, but during this period in my life she just made it hard on me. I guess it had something to do with being a young person. When I got married and moved out my sister went on to have her own bedroom, and here was I returning home and asking that she let me have a part it. She simply did not want to share her bedroom with me. I'm sure she probably thinks about it once in a while now and wonders, "What did I do to my own sister?"

I remember the first night that I slept in my mother's house. I was having pains because of the fall in the court. I was pregnant, and my mother told my sister to share the bed with me. She said no. My mother had to pull a mattress from one of the other rooms, and I ended up sleeping on a mattress on the floor. I cried all night until about four in the morning when I started having sharp pains and realized that I was losing the baby. My sister or the situation at my mother's house didn't have anything to do with the death of my baby. That resulted from the way I was treated in the courtroom. In any event, after this my mother got me a twin-sized bed and put it in the living room for me.

Four months into my marriage the world stopped circulating as I had planned. Its rotation was following a course opposite from the one I had drawn up. Overall, I felt that in the blink of an eye I had lost everything. Everything had been taken from me. I lost a child; my husband was gone. I didn't know if he was going to come home so everything was very new. The security of my own home was taken from me as well. We had been married for only four months, and it was very hard.

From that point on I started getting stronger. I was suffering, but I was having to find strength to continue with life. It was difficult, but I knew that I had to carry myself.

Then I realized very quickly that things were not going to change. While he was serving time, my husband got into a lot of fights because there are all kinds of gang members in jail fighting for control. He was always put to the test of proving himself. And he was not one to walk away from any fight. He would fight with anybody that challenged him. It got to the point that, every week when I went to visit him, he was some place else. He was constantly being changed or transferred from one cell to another. I would find him with some bruises, and I would immediately ask him to tell me what was going on, and he would simply say, "Don't worry, don't worry." But I did worry.

It was all very confusing because there was nothing that I could do. I was so young that I didn't have the knowledge or the understanding that I now have for helping him. I thought that no one was going to listen to a fifteen-year-old kid. I didn't know what to do or where to go for help.

My husband was let out in six months. I never expected that he was going to be away from me for such a long time. The way he was freed was crazy. I remember that, when we went into the courtroom to begin the proceedings for the trial, I noticed everyone was nervous. We were told to step outside the courtroom, and I saw that the sheriff's police were looking out of the windows and just walking around. For a minute I thought that someone had escaped or something terrible had happened outside.

When we returned to the courtroom I noticed that there wasn't a jury. I was expecting to see one; after all, my husband was going to be tried by a jury. There was only the judge. Our attorney came and sat in front of me and told me: "They're going to let them go—don't get hysterical. Tell the family not to get really rowdy. Everything is going to be okay." It didn't click. My mind was so tuned into the trial that what the attorney was telling me didn't register. My husband's mother leaned over and asked me in Spanish, "What did the lawyer say?" I told her, "They're going to let the guys out." It was only at this time that I came to realize the news of my husband's release. And all of a sudden they came out. They were happy; they all had big smiles. The judge made an announcement: "The jury was dismissed because the witnesses have taken back their testimonies. You're free to go." There was no trial. It was over. It was amazing.

When my husband finally came home he was angrier. He was

trying to change his life around, but the gang activity followed him, and that's when he said that he wasn't going to stop. Losing a baby for a case that wasn't his fault left him more bitter, to the extent that was beyond control.

Although I can say we had some very special moments, it's also true that I shared him with the streets. When we talk about these things now he often laughs because he believes things weren't that way. After he served those first six months I felt like I had a part-time husband. I really believe that, if I really counted first for him, if I was the first priority in his life, he would have been home with me. Perhaps he would not be where he is today. The only reason he's there now is because he was so visible. He was out in the streets at all times. Sometimes he would stay out until three or four in the morning. I never knew from one day to the next what was going to happen. When you spend your time hanging out with guys there are only two possible outcomes: death or incarceration. So, he thinks about it now and says, "You're right." But I ended up sharing him with his friends, and I realized it was a way of life.

I was always telling him in a positive way things that I thought would change our lives and the whole situation. For example, I remember suggesting to him that we go to live in Puerto Rico. We had enough money to build a house there. Even though the two of us were not raised here, I thought that, since Puerto Rico was our homeland, we would enjoy life there. In my mind I thought Puerto Rico has this magnificent weather and overall peaceful atmosphere; this was going to be our getaway. We were going to begin from point one, in our land, where everybody was the same. These were some of the wonderful thoughts and ideas I used to share with him. But he said no. He refused to consider my ideas, and it was primarily because of the guys. There was, and still is, a bond with the guys and the organization.

I felt hurt to hear him say no to the ideas that I thought could help us solve the situation. I felt like he didn't want to try a new life or a new environment. I was convinced that he didn't want to give anything a try. He would always say, "We're going to do that, but not now." Everything I told him, ideas about moving, were always responded to in the same fashion: "Later" and "We'll do that another time."

I had a choice. I could have walked away. I didn't have to remain in this relationship. I remember one day I was telling my mother-in-law, while he was on the corner: "This is it. I can't take it. I'm going to leave." This was about the third year of our marriage. She ran and told him to come and find out what was wrong because I was planning to leave. But it didn't faze him because in his mind he was so secure. He knew that I would be there no matter what.

In a way I felt upset knowing that he was so sure of himself. I guess he knew me better than I knew myself. He always said that he knew that he picked the right woman. But when I would hear that I would laugh and tell him that he picked a fool. Actually, it was that he knew that I took marriage very seriously. I was upset that he wouldn't take me seriously. Maybe he thought about it. He just never admitted that he was concerned. Maybe, if I would have left him, it would have worked, but I stuck it out.

I don't feel sorry that I didn't walk out on him. I guess in my mind I was thinking, "If I walk out, I might lose him." I was stuck between a rock and a hard place. I knew that, if I left, because of his machismo, his reaction was going to be "Fine, let her leave." When I say this to him now he doesn't agree. He says that he would have come looking for me. But I didn't see it that way because he's such a fighter, such a strong head, very independent. I couldn't see him at that time crumbling because a woman left.

I was afraid to be alone too. In our culture you find a number of people who look at a divorced woman or man and might say: "That's a good woman, and that's a good man. They probably had a failure, and they are entitled to other changes and opportunities in life." But then there's a greater percentage that feels, "Well, she's already divorced, so, hey, she could give it up at any time." I didn't want to have to go through that. So, I decided to stick it out and try to work at the marriage.

In addition, I wanted my marriage to work so bad. I wanted to be the exception to the rule. That was another major reason why it was important for me to stay in the marriage and make it work. When we got married I remember one of my high school teachers, who knew my husband, telling me: "You're not gonna make it; you're so different from him. I'll give you one year." That was so engraved in my mind. I decided that I was going to defeat all odds. I was going to do it. I still hear myself saying: "I'm going to make it. I'm going to show all those people that I'm going to make my marriage work."

That was my way of thinking. It made me feel stronger. I was so stubborn to make our marriage work; I was going to accomplish it whether from the inside, where he is now, or from here, together, on the outside.

Lourdes's husband's initial incarceration caused the two of them to stop attending high school. Because he was now serving time, Lourdes's husband could not continue going to school. Lourdes, on the other hand, decided to withdraw because, she felt, her husband's needs required constant attention. Lourdes also anticipated the strain of being in school under these conditions.

Because of his record, once out of prison Lourdes's husband was not permitted to return to the job he had previously held. He became embittered, feeling profound animosity toward individuals who were judging him on the basis of his six months' experience in jail. As a result, he turned more and more to the gang for emotional support. Within the gang he found those opportunities he believed he was now being denied as a former inmate—in particular, a job.

Because of his first case, neither one of us graduated from high school. I didn't like having to drop out of school because I really enjoyed school. I just couldn't cope with our circumstances. Everything was happening while my husband and I were both in high school.

After leaving school it's so difficult to return. I couldn't go back because my friends were there, and I didn't want to have to face them and tell them what had happened. It would have been so humiliating. At one time I was doing so well in school. I got married, and I was about to have a baby. Then, suddenly, I lost my baby; my husband was incarcerated. I knew that it would have been very stressful attending school under those conditions. There was no way I could have studied. And I knew that my friends in school as well as the teachers would question me. I just didn't want to talk about what had happened. My pride couldn't let me go back. So, I just went to work in a candy factory until he would come home.

In the case of my husband, after serving the six-month term, he had to attend school in the evenings to finish up. He was not able to graduate with his class. Before the trial he was working in a maintenance job, but after his release he couldn't go back to that job because, no matter how many letters were written saying that the whole thing was a mistake, they wouldn't take him back. People were being judge and jury, refusing to give him a fair chance. They would not listen and give him an opportunity. Since my husband was gone for six months, they probably thought about what was going to happen next.

In my opinion people always look at the outside of a person and judge him on that basis. How often have we heard the expression "You can't judge a book by its cover"? I couldn't agree more. You must read the book and discover how it really is. You can't possibly develop an opinion of a book on the basis of its title. People should start by saying, "Let's see who this person is." Instead, they always jump the gun, and in the case of my husband I felt I was the only one protecting him, the only one saying, "No, that's not what he is really about."

I guess I can understand. But I also think that, if they had given him and others like him an opportunity, they would have turned out differently. But these young men realize that, since they have an X on their backs, they will never be looked at positively by anyone. So, they figure: "What's the use? I'll go to the streets and do what I'm used to; after all, the streets never reject me." And this is what this society needs to look at. It needs to provide people with opportunities to move forward and to prove themselves. But, if it continues to close the door because of a mistake committed by a person, what's going to come of us? Who doesn't make a mistake today?

So, a lot of discouragement came upon my husband because of everything he had experienced. He enjoyed his job and was making good money. But he couldn't get his job back. He felt that justice was not served and that the only way of making money would be through the streets. He wanted to do things the correct way, but suddenly all of the doors closed on him because of mistakes. People didn't want to believe what really had happened. Instead, they judged him and refused to give him the opportunity to get his life in order.

As a result, he became very rebellious. He was innocent; he didn't commit the crime, but we had lost everything. He got more involved in gang activities. I saw us going backward. There was nothing I could say that could change him, and I just watched everything crumble.

He was organizing more, forming the guys. There was more of an organization developing out there. There might be some people who do not agree, but I would say that in earlier times the gang was more like a bunch of guys hanging out. But after that [after getting out of prison and when drugs started entering the community] the shootings and fighting for territory were all conducted through the organization. Things were being done with more planning. It came down to the issue of who was going to rule what: "This territory belonged to me, this corner belonged to me—so you guys better not even think of trying to take it from us." Then the individual gang member who was more strong-headed and more forceful, the one who got his point across, was the leader. I don't mean the guy that was more physically strong but, rather, the one who could voice an opinion and have others respect it. My husband became that person. He was very influential. He was able to convince the guys that they could do this and that and make money. And that sounded so inviting, because these guys were all in the same situation. He was the one that prevailed as their leader.

So, my husband started organizing more. The scam was building up quite heavily, and the police just wanted to get rid of it, no matter what. They wanted him because he was a leader and because he wouldn't stay quiet. The police tried picking him up on the corner for drug involvement or for anything. They tried fabricating case after case to make sure that they could arrest him. And my husband is the type that you can kill him, and he's not going to talk. So, that's what happened. They would pick him up for something minor and sometimes really stupid, but he would simply refuse to answer when they questioned him. And, because of that, they would charge him and lock him up. He was forever in and out of 26th Street and California [the county jail]. I would stay up late at night wondering if he was ever going to come home. I would wonder if I was going to get a call.

Lourdes was well aware of her husband's involvement in the gang. She also knew that he was heavily involved in drug distribution and marketing; after all, money was always available for her use. Although she was informed, there was little Lourdes could do to turn things in the direction she wanted. Yet she maintained her dignity and power by not allowing her husband's drug dealing and use to go on in her house. For Lourdes control over house matters became symbolic of her power.

I didn't give much thought to what my husband was doing because I was to myself making sure that my material needs (in terms of my home and finances) were being met. If I needed to buy something, the money was always there, so I didn't have to worry.

I didn't like how things were being done, but I didn't have anything to say. The way I saw it at the time was that I didn't have a choice. I always had the faith that things were going to get better. I chose this kind of life, and I decided to stick it out.

This is not to say that I didn't express my opinion. I always told my husband and his friends how I felt. I remember one conversation I had with his friends at the house one time. They were reading the paper about a shooting that had taken place and they were making fun of how the family of the victim was grieving. I realized that these guys were high, but, still, they were laughing. So, I told them off. I said to them: "How could you? That's pain. It could have been any one of you guys, and we could be the ones crying right now. What's wrong with you? Why don't you understand?" My husband's reaction was "Leave it alone."

I was angry when this incident occurred. I walked away from the guys to my room. I slammed the door of the room and locked myself in it. I was frustrated with their ignorance. They had this attitude that they were invincible. They believed that killing and dying were things that happened to others but not to them. I just wanted to turn them inside out. Whenever they saw me upset and acting this way they would simply leave the house. They had respect for me. That was their way of showing it. Yet I knew how they were thinking, and it bothered me a great deal.

In spite of all of the things that he was experiencing, my husband didn't give up. He finally found a job in a tool factory, and after about two years he started attending college for computers. And, just as he was going to receive his first degree in data processing, that is when this [next disruption] came up.

I was working during the time I was living with my mother. Although I was making minimum wage, something like three or four dollars an hour, I was able to save most of it. I didn't pay rent or the other expenses that come with living in your own apartment or house.

To some extent, after he served the first six months at the Cook County Jail and got out when he beat the case, our lives were picking up after a couple years. We had the down payment on a house in Bolingbrook [a suburb southwest of Chicago]. Two weeks before we were about to move out he was shot right in my presence, in front of our home.

The day he was shot was really unexpected. I was returning from visiting my brother, who was incarcerated and was about to be released from an eighteen-month sentence. On our way back from the institution my car broke down. It was a three-hour drive. I called my husband, and he came out to help us. When he got there the car started working. So, he decided to drive my car, while I drove his. We came back and picked up my father, and we all went out to eat. My husband was in real good spirits.

After dinner we came home. My husband parked his car real quickly, while it took me a little bit of time to park. Actually, I was having problems parking because the space was difficult getting into. When my husband saw what I was doing he called out to me. He said, "No, Lourdes, you're doing it wrong." It was then that I heard the shots. He was shot twice with a .30-30 rifle that almost left him for dead.

When I heard the shots I got a piercing sound in my ear. It was a very strong sound. I thought that an electric cable had fallen onto the street. I didn't think the noice was that of gunshots, because of the sound. I got out of the car, and I fell to my knees, and I told him to stay there. I had no idea that he had been shot because he fell on his back. He didn't close his eyes. He was looking at me. He didn't talk because the first shot got his neck and got his vocal chords. He couldn't tell me he was hurt. Then another shot rang out. I was frozen. I tried to look and move, but I couldn't. Finally, I realized that he was hurt. I started screaming, and people came out with blankets, and someone called the ambulance.

On the way to the hospital I looked at him—I didn't believe this was happening. He was going to die. I didn't think he'd make it. I was so confused. I didn't know what to do. I just couldn't talk. His friends were informed of what had happened, and they were told to come to the hospital. At the hospital the room was filled with people. His friends and everyone else were asking me questions, and I couldn't tell them anything because I couldn't see anything. I felt like a blind person. I didn't have any vision. I could not see anyone or anything, except for what had happened.

I was also resentful of two policemen who got involved in the case, because all they wanted to know was whether my husband had a gun or not. I was so angry that I told them that, if he'd had a gun, he wouldn't be where he is because he would have defended himself. They just walked away. I discovered later that the two policemen had gotten into our car and searched it. I don't know how they did it, but they did enter our car. When they didn't find anything there they tried getting into our apartment, but the landlord didn't let them in. I'm thankful for the landlord. What right did these cops have to get into people's homes? If anything, they should have gone to find who shot my husband, but they didn't care. They just wanted my husband out of the way. I'm certain that they were hoping that he would not make it.

It was a true nightmare. Afterward, my husband was taken into intensive care. He spent a month there.

The first shot got his neck from one end to the next, and the next bullet hit his leg. The bullet that went into the leg came out through his thigh. That affected his intestines. The doctors also told me that he might not be able to talk again because the bullet that got him on the throat had injured his vocal chords. But I knew that he was strong willed, and after a month he began to talk.

As soon as my husband was hospitalized, I had to take a leave from work. He was in the hospital for over a month, and I spent the entire time by his bedside. I was afraid that something would happen when I wasn't there. So, I decided to stay there every minute of the day and night. The nurses were wonderful. I literally lived in the hospital, going home just for an hour or so to bathe and come right back. We would fall asleep together watching television—him in his bed and me in my chair. I don't know how many other wives would have done that for their husband, but I didn't want the nurses to do anything for him. I fed him, changed his clothes, and gave him a bath. And those were moments that made us grow together in such a bond that you can't break up.

My husband loved the fact that I decided to spend all this time with him. We were going through this ordeal together. I remember that, about the fourth week, I came into the room to find him with a big smile on his face. Up to this time he had communicated with me through written notes, but this day he motioned to me to come closer to him. When I did he said, "Lourdes, I love you." It was beautiful. Those were the first words he said when he began talking.

I was expecting that, since my husband had been so near the door of death, once he was released from the hospital that he would stop [being involved with the gang]. The reverse happened. After he got better there was no stopping him. Since he has always been a strong-headed fighter, he wasn't going to let anyone get away with what they had done. He said that they were going to kill me while I was in his car; I told him not to worry, to leave it in the hands of God, but he wouldn't listen to me. So, we moved back to the [Division Street] neighborhood; my mother left us her apartment, while she went to live in the basement apartment.

This time he never went anywhere alone. He was always with his friends or with a cousin who came to live with us. They left and came home together. They were like his bodyguards. I felt a little secure knowing that he wasn't alone, but it was hard. I didn't feel it was worth going after the person that had caused this pain and hurt. His friends were really the ones who said that something had to be done, that they had to avenge the shooting—my husband didn't have to do anything, because there were others willing. He didn't listen. I had many sleepless nights. I kept hearing the shots he was hit with, and I just wanted to leave Chicago. But he wouldn't leave.

The morning he got picked up for good I got up feeling like something real bad was about to happen to him. I went to work, and about eleven that morning my mother called and told me to come home because my husband had been arrested.

Since we were living back in the neighborhood, he was well known there. So, even though the murder for which he was arrested happened on the other side of town, the police came over to our side—the police do that all the time. They go to known gang turfs to question gang members. In the case of my husband, he was stopped while driving home with some friends. Imagine that! A car filled with young Puerto Rican men at a time when the police were looking to make an arrest. Of course, a case was fabricated against my husband. The specifics of the allegations are not very significant as far as I am concerned. What really matters is that a group of men was made to suffer because the system needed to protect and cover itself. Again, this has been such a common occurence in our neighborhood.

It took a year for my husband's case to come to trial. He was being held at Cook County Jail again. But this time things were harder because he was in and out of the Cook County Hospital [the city's only public hospital], since his injuries from the gunshot wounds had not fully healed. He was in a very delicate health condition, and it was very frustrating for both of us. I couldn't take care of him. I knew that he was living in very unsanitary conditions;

it wasn't clean there. Sometimes I would go to see him at the hospital because he had been taken there due to infections he contracted in the unclean cells where he was kept.

The court and the state's attorney wanted my husband behind bars real bad. They decided to resort to anything to get him because they thought he had gotten away with so many other things. And he might have, but not with killing. He was charged falsely with the killing. They wanted him off the streets because they thought he had such a big influence in the neighborhood, which he did. Although the case was not gang related—it was supposed to have been a murder case—the state's attorney made sure that the judge and jury knew that my husband and the other guys were involved in gangs, that the jury knew that these individuals were from Humboldt Park, the most gang-infested and vicious area in the city, and that my husband was a known gang leader. When the case got weak they got an inmate who was with my husband at the county jail to say that my husband had made arrangements to have the state's attorney killed. The same witness also made the allegation that my husband's friends had robbed a train full of ammunition. I was thinking, "Are these people insane?" If something like that had happened, it would had been all over the newspapers and television.

This was the image of my husband and his friends that became ingrained in the head of the judge. In addition, when the witnesses first testified they said that they saw four individuals running with ski masks on. That was it. A year later, at the trial, all of them described everything the guys were wearing, including the color socks they had on.

It was very much a political case because it was during the time of elections that the state's attorney, who is now the mayor, was saying that he was going to put away gang members and drug dealers, no matter what. It was really an outrageous case.

When the judge handed down the sentence my husband got a

seventy-year prison term. One other individual got fifty years. The other one just got the forty-year maximum sentence. Here are three people sentenced for the murder of one person, with no evidence; the evidence presented was all manufactured. The only thing they had were eyewitness accounts by people who at first indicated that they didn't know anything. Even the sentences they were given were so different that you have to wonder how objective the whole decision was. One person got this sentence, another got this one. What was going on? I guess you can only wonder!

In my mind I was anticipating the best possible outcome for the trial. For an entire year I had waited for the trial, feeling very confident because he didn't do it, and I thought that justice would prevail. I came to the trial to return home with my husband.

And then the guilty verdict was read. My initial reaction to the guilty verdict was shock. I thought, "Here we go again." I had high hopes; everything was going to turn out for the best this time. The guilty verdict took a lot out of me. I was devastated. I wasn't expecting it, even though my family was telling me to prepare for the worst. So, when the guilty verdict was read I was shocked. I stood there frozen. I couldn't do anything. I just looked at my husband and saw that frozen look on his face. Here was this big glass between us, and we couldn't console one another. I thought: "What's going to happen? We're not going to be together for a long, long time."

I immediately began to feel a deep pain and a feeling of hate toward the courts and the judicial system. I hated everything about them. I thought that they went out of their way to prove the case against my husband and the other members of the gang. It seemed like there was no stopping them in their quest for a conviction. I'm sure they were happy. I was very bitter. Now I look at things differently. But at the time I didn't think they treated my husband's case fairly. Even the attorney who represented my husband was convinced that my husband was this terrible person. In my opinion he didn't fight the case effectively in defending my husband. The attorney never told me that he felt that my husband was guilty; he always acted very sympathetic. It got to the point that, no matter what, my husband wasn't going to win.

I felt destroyed and humiliated. I felt that someone took the floor out from under me, that someone had taken everything, the last breath out of me. His friends and our family followed me home from the trial because they thought I was going to *lose it*, or worse. I just wanted to eliminate anything that had to do with gangs. At that moment I had hate. I hated their relationship and the love that they had and felt for this gang. Because of this, I felt, they did not see the pain they can cause a wife or a mother. When I got home I was like a viscious dog. I told them to get away. I was very resentful and very hateful. I locked myself in my room. I didn't want to talk or see anybody. The first things I saw when I got into the house were some statues that my husband absolutely loved; they represented symbols of the gang. I quickly realized that because of the gang activity this was happening to me. I destroyed the statues. I wanted to destroy the gang. The whole perception of colors [colors of gang's clothing as well as its particular signs and symbols]—I was suffering, and I wanted someone else to hurt. Anything that related to the colors I wanted to get rid of.

I went into my husband's closet and just took anything that was associated with the gang and broke it up. I just needed to get this hurt out somehow. People just looked at me as if I was crazy. I think it worked. My inner feelings were feeling better. After this I just sat in my room and cried for I don't know how long. It was hours. The house was filled with people, but I couldn't see anybody. I was so drained. In my mind I could only think, "Just leave me alone."

In the meantime people kept drifting in and out. A lot of his friends came over, and I guess they wanted to show me their support—to let me know they were there and that everything was going to be okay. But everything was not okay. I didn't want to hear them say that everything was going to be okay, because it was not— not for a long time, I thought.

I still see these guys today. They have always been respectful. Every time they see me they give me a hug and kiss. Their view is that I'm so good because I'm fighting for their leader. So, again, they relate one thing with the other. They fail to realize that Lourdes is a good person, and what she is doing is something *she* wants to do, not out of fear for him but because she really cares for him. One time I told my husband, "Don't you think that I'm doing this for you because you are a leader. I'm waiting for you because I love you. Don't even think it's because I fear you or anyone out there." See, some of these guys can't see what true love is. They love one another; they love the gang—but they can't understand the love of a family, as they see themselves as a family.

I'm talking about the younger members, because, while they were in prison, their wives decided not to stand by them. So, they think that I'm doing this because he's the leader and that I have to do it this way. I've told several that I do it because I want to. I've learned to love them all in a special way. I never stop talking to them, reminding them of what I'm going through and not to make the same mistake [as my husband, being involved with the gang] because other people are going to hurt just as much.

When my husband was found guilty and sentenced my mother-in-law and I were upset with each other. In the early years I felt like she used to think that I took her son away. So, there were always little spats. We would argue sometimes about the dumbest things, nothing really important. There were times when I defended my husband from things she would say—these were the kinds of things that would get her upset with me.

She never went to court during the entire course. It wasn't that she didn't want to be there, but she knew that I was. She knew that everything was going to be alright as long as I was attending to the case. She decided to remain at home and pray with candles; this was the ritual she followed.

But a day after the trial and the sentencing one of his aunts came over and asked me to go with her to see her sister. I said yes. At that time my mother-in-law was the only person I wanted to see. I felt we had something in common. We were both going through this enormous pain, that no one else knew what it was like. I walked into the house and found her lying in bed. We hugged and started crying. We kept reassuring one another that everything was going to be fine.

The two of us, my mother-in-law and I, developed a bond that no one would ever break. From this point on a ritual began whereby I go to visit her every week. During the visits we talk about many things, but one thing we never fail to cover is how to fight this case. That's where we are at today.

CHAPTER

3

Getting into the Drug Business

Like many other poor neighborhoods in U.S. cities, the Division Street area, where Lourdes was raised, became the site of a drug epidemic during the 1970s and 1980s. It came storming through the neighborhood, affecting many of its residents. Drug problems plagued the young people, in particular. Many of them were involved in using or selling at least one kind of drug, principally marijuana and cocaine.

The male youth gang became the leading formal organization around which drugs were marketed and distributed at the street level. Numerous youth gangs sprang up throughout the Division Street area, giving this community the infamous distinction of being one of the most gang-saturated areas in the entire city. Division Street also developed a reputation as a community in which drugs were readily available, making it attractive to customers from the neighborhood as well as those from areas outside. For the youth gang this meant securing control over some part of the drug-dealing market within the community, some turf. Youngsters from the neighborhood were being recruited for participation in the many different and competing

*ngs. Gang leaders clearly understood that the more numerous the gang,
the more likely it could succeed in overtaking others and controlling drug
distribution and sales. A fierce and ongoing war began over control of the
various neighborhood drug dealing "turfs."*

*Gang participation was introduced to neighborhood youngsters as a vehicle for making money. While they understood gang membership involved
fighting against opposition gangs, they believed they were being recruited
"to work" for the gang in its drug-dealing operations. Never before had the
youth from the Division Street area been so vigorously sought after to fill
jobs (albeit of an illegal nature). Given the marginal, low-paying jobs
they—and their family members and friends—held generally, young boys
from* el barrio *developed a positive view toward the job of drug dealing; in
their minds this line of work represented their ticket to "making it."*

*What young people and other residents of Division Street were responding to was societal neglect, best observed by the removal of manufacturing
work from communities such as theirs since the 1960s. Jobs in factories and
manufacturing plants, which had anchored earlier generations of immigrants and their families in established neighborhoods by offering stable
employment, now moved from major U.S. cities to suburban areas and to the
South and the Third World, where nonunionized workers could be readily
hired at low wages. As expected, more and more inner-city residents became
unemployed.*

*Very quickly these individuals began to understand the implications of
these socioeconomic changes: they had to learn to develop entrepreneurial
skills in order to survive, since they had been left virtually on their own,
without conventional resources or means with which to make a living.
Within this context it did not take long for certain individuals to come along
and take advantage of the vulnerability of inner-city residents, filling their
communities with drugs and advertising drug dealing as the fastest way to
"earn a buck." That individuals from Division Street and other such communities were lured by the prospects is understandable, given the paucity of
"legitimate" jobs.*

Lourdes's teenage years were spent within this context of gangs and drugs, including the brief time she spent actually living with her husband in the "outside world." Much of her way of life, her ways of thinking and acting were directly shaped by this social and cultural environment.

When I was a teenager most of my friends, my brother, and I had jobs through the different summer programs sponsored by the city's Department of Human Resources. The aim of these programs was to employ youngsters who were from poor families. This was a way of preventing us from hanging out and getting into trouble. Nearly all the young people in our neighborhood qualified for these jobs because their families were low income. Around this time my parents were divorced, and my mother had to go on public assistance.

Most of us liked the jobs because we were pretty much out in the streets, working with our friends doing cleanup work. Other people were hired to do work in offices, typing and doing secretarial kinds of duties. Others worked with younger kids in day camps, the YMCA [Young Men's Christian Association], or in school daycare programs.

There were times when we were taken to the sites where lunch was served to summer school children. We would help to serve the lunches. We would talk to the children. They, in turn, had a chance to meet and talk to individuals who were older and who were working. I always thought that, indirectly, we were serving as their role models. What a wonderful idea. I don't even know if officials from the program knew what they were doing, but the job was giving opportunities to young people to see teenagers who were working.

I have always loved children. They represent our future, and we must try very hard to serve as positive role models for them. Young people need individuals who are willing to nurture them or simply to make a good impression. This was something I always wanted to do. The jobs we had through the summer program enabled us to come before children and show them that we were serious and together and so could they.

That was fun. It didn't seem like a job or chore. It was always a good feeling because we were doing something for other people, especially for the young children of the neighborhood. We were not sitting around with nothing to do. We were getting things accomplished, even though sometimes we were the ones who dropped the garbage on the streets or dirtied up the parks. Of course, we were responsible for cleaning up our own garbage. We also were told to remove the paint from the garage doors that some of us had graffitied.

In a way this line of work provided us with good experiences and good feelings about contributing to the upkeep of the community. It made us feel like we belonged and that we needed to become responsible for what was happening to things around us, in our neighborhood. The work made us appreciate the neighborhood more. We felt like this was ours and we were responsible for what happens to it. We were very young, yet, from seeing others throwing bottles and other garbage on what we had cleaned, we learned to appreciate our streets, sidewalks, alleys, and buildings. So, in a way the job opened up our eyes to what was happening, to what was important. It made us aware that the environment must be preserved and kept clean all the time. How can people like to live in a community when it is always filled with garbage? To make people become devoted we must maintain the community looking clean.

On the other hand, there were not enough jobs for people to even begin to think about making it. We couldn't get very far with these kinds of jobs. They could only provide so much, since we couldn't continue working after the summer. There were jobs in the local hot dog stand or the restaurant, but we didn't want to do that. After working in jobs that we enjoyed during the summer, when the school year started we were returned to doing the kinds of jobs we had always been told belonged to Puerto Ricans and other Latinos. We felt these jobs were demeaning. We were not going to school to slave in restaurants. It's interesting because the summer jobs we had involved cleaning and sweeping around the neighborhood and the park. But we looked at these jobs in a different way. We were doing something that was essential for maintaining our community. The jobs in the restaurants called for people to get dirty without seeing any direct benefits going to our neighborhood. We never worked directly with people. We were there to turn hamburgers and hot dogs.

I remember working in this hot dog stand once. The owner was nice, but he was also very rude. I wanted to work in the front where I could greet the customers because I always have liked working directly with people. Instead, he had me working in the back, taking out the garbage, sweeping the floors, or making hot dogs. I was about to quit the job one day when an order was returned to me because the customer didn't want something that I had put on the hot dog. As I was getting ready to dispose of the order, the owner came to the back and told me to just get rid of the bun. He told me to simply clean up the hot dog and to put it in a different bun. I thought, "You can't treat people like that, especially since they are my people," so the next day I quit. I couldn't work there after witnessing how our own were being treated.

These experiences left me and many of the neighborhood youngsters with a bad taste. Many of us decided not to bother with those kinds of jobs. Our parents did not want us near those places. Of course, there were other youngsters from the neighborhood who had to work, regardless of the job and pay. They did not have a choice. Their families were desperate.

So, what happened was that many of the young people started getting into the drug-dealing scene. Instead of cooking and turning hamburgers at Mickey Ds [McDonald's], they opted for a new enterprise. And all of a sudden everywhere you went there were the drugs. Drugs took over our neighborhood. Drugs could be found as far as you could see. You couldn't walk a block without someone offering you something.

On my street about ten of the twenty families were involved with drugs. Everyone was using; everyone was selling. Those who didn't sell it were using it. Those who weren't using it were looking out for those who were selling it. It was like a sickness because some people were experiencing a great deal of pain. At the same time others were making money from the sickness and pain. It was such an irony, but, because we were so young, we did or could not see the whole picture. Very little attention was paid to those who were becoming sick; after all money was being made.

The women were involved too. They would hold the drugs for their husband, boyfriend, brother, or even for just a friend. There was a time in the early 1970s that male police officers were the ones assigned to ride around and patrol the neighborhood, and without a female officer they could not search the women. The guys on the streets knew this and used the girls to hold their stuff. The women were just as aware, and holding the stuff became a way for them to earn money. It was not until the police got wind of this that they realized they needed to have policewomen in the cars in the neighborhood.

People were selling directly from their apartments; others sold from the streets. You never knew where it was coming from. But one thing is certain: everyone was trying to make it big. It was surprising when at times I would find out who was involved. My reaction was always, "Oh, really, that person?" Young people saw a few others getting into riches almost overnight. At least this is how it appeared, and they wanted a piece of what these other guys were doing. They were going to make it big time. It also appeared like people were not afraid; they were really desperate not to have cared. Of course, they did not want to end up in prison, but what else was there for them to do? It was simple: people wanted to make money, and drugs were the only way to make it.

I was about fourteen or so when, during an afterschool program, my brother and I came to the realization that the person who was running the program was using the facilities to deal drugs; he was probably doing other things there too. This guy was selling drugs right after work hours were over, when we were supposed to have gone home. Young guys there were also smoking on the premises. I saw all of this with my own two eyes. I remember seeing a marijuana plant growing in the back of the place and asking my brother, "What is that?" He told me what it was. "It's a marijuana plant," he said. I was shocked. I didn't know what to do or say. I had seen news reports about these kinds of situations but never from my neighborhood. Now they were happening right where I was, right in my face. I couldn't believe they were actually true. But, of course, they were as true as all the other things that were taking place in every street and many homes in our community. Drugs were making people do crazy things.

I'm certain that low-income neighborhoods are targets of drug distribution and selling because we are more susceptible. We have always been a community of poor people. We are hard working, but we are also poor. Sometimes we don't have total control over our own lives because we don't possess the resources necessary for making decisions that will better us. So, at times we have to rely on the influence of other people, and oftentimes these people don't really care about what happens to the people from neighborhoods like mine. As long as we produce what they want, they are satisfied. Of course, we always end up paying the consequences. Our people are the ones who end up with the court record, with the police reports. Our people are the ones who end up in jail. These are the consequences we must pay because we must sell our work to those who are more than willing to hire us in their businesses.

All of this happened to our people in particular. Young people in my neighborhood were being offered something they never had. They were all young and eager to make that money, and here were these other people offering them hundreds of dollars that could be used to obtain those things that they only would see on television.

For a long time these young people had been shown those things that people considered fundamental to life. They also saw the luxury items in store displays. Before their eyes were the name-brand clothing and the gold, the more visible of all the items they could buy or possess.

But these young people never had the means to obtain these items; they were from low-income families. They kept asking: "Why can't we have the things that other people have? We should be entitled to acquire these items the same way as the next person." Of course, when the drug storm came these young people were swept by it. They went for it; they got into drugs big time.

How could they have turned away? They were very aware of the risk and danger involved in drug dealing, but they were aware of the dollar signs as well. These guys began to think that this was the way they were going to support their families. Others even thought of ideas about buying a house; they were going to use the profits from drug dealing to purchase themselves and their family a house. And that's what happened.

Some guy, some person, someone with mega-money, came into our neighborhood and preyed on the eagerness of our young people. You need to have big money to purchase large amounts of drugs for distribution. Our guys, many of whom were young boys, didn't have that kind of cash. Instead, they became hired labor, doing the most risky part of the business for the drug-dealing gang. They were told that, if they were good at their job, for example, not allowing the police to bust them, they could earn big money. That was enough to convince many to get into the business.

At that time my opinion of what was taking place around me was that it was terrible and bad. I knew that drug use and dealing were harmful for our youngsters. Even then I recognized that our young women and men were being used and abused. I came to know that it was our young people who were having to pay for the consequences of dealing. You never would see the big wheels, the big dealers; these guys never got locked up. The ones that could always be found were the street dealers.

Then there was the group of people that only used drugs. They did not get into drugs in search of economic payoffs; rather, drugs offered them a psychological escape from their very difficult realities. When one of our young people, whether a man or woman, is high on drugs, that person doesn't have to worry about his or her problems. The drug is the answer to the problems. In the mind of that person there is no better solution to a life that has been filled with lies and illusions. That person begins to rely on drugs for taking trips that take him or her so high and far that all of the injustices of the world turn invisible.

For many of these individuals drugs were a way to deal with life itself. They serve as constant reminders of the difficulties involved in coping with life. Not everyone can cope; we use different mechanisms and methods. Unfortunately, for some people in poor communities drugs have served as the mechanism for getting them through. I see many of these individuals constantly high, and they will not get off that high. I understand about their problems, but I'm convinced that they need to find a better solution. They are really fooling themselves in believing that, by using drugs, their problems will go away. How can one person get high for a couple of hours, knowing that afterward his or her problems and other situations will still be there? For the life of me I can't understand this logic, but they did.

The couples that I was around were pretty much into smoking marijuana. The ladies smoked with their husbands. They were escaping together from the conditions that surrounded them. They were taking high trips that would take them to a world different from the one in which they lived. And, even if the pscyhological escape lasted for a few minutes, they thought it was all worth it.

They didn't see anything wrong with smoking. They did it, and to them it was as normal as smoking a pack of Kools [brand of cigarettes]. They had seen the hippies from the 1960s smoke their heads off without anything happening to them. So, people had seen the ease with which the hippies smoked. They began to believe that there was no danger in smoking and doing cocaine; after all, an entire generation of young, white, middle-class people had gone berserk using drugs ten years earlier, and nothing had happened to them.

One particular case I recall well involved one of my closest friends, who got hooked on cocaine. This friend came over to my house one day asking me for money for drugs. She even suggested that we both try it. I think that this was her way of trying to convince me to give her the money to buy the stuff. After seeing the way she was, the way she was behaving, that's when I said no to both of her requests. My friend enjoyed doing cocaine so much. She thought there was nothing wrong about taking it. To her doing coke was something very normal. In any event, at that point I knew she had a serious problem. To this day she is still using. To me drug abuse is drug abuse. No matter how a person looks at it, if that person claims to be using drugs for recreational reasons, as far as I'm concerned, that's drug abuse.

From then on I came to the conclusion that drugs were not for me. I became terrified by cocaine. I saw it as such an easy drug to carry around and to take. A person could hide it in many places, none of which could be found if that person was really good. Another thing about cocaine was that it did not take very long to take. And it wasn't painful, like when people shoot up [drugs such as heroin or cocaine]. It didn't have a smell like when you smoke marijuana; when you smoke the smell itself informs others of what you're doing. I had tried smoking marijuana, but I never liked it. It had such a dry taste, and then it makes me hungry; I didn't like it. In fact, I did not want to mess with any kind of drugs.

Lourdes's husband did not share her views about drug use. Like others described by Lourdes as having fallen victim to the psychological escape offered by drugs, her husband was a heavy user, although she did not characterize him as a drug abuser.

Although these were my views and attitudes toward drugs, for my husband things were different. He was one of those who fell victim to the epidemic. All of the time my husband was out here in the world he used drugs. He did drugs all the time, though he was very careful about the amount he used. He wasn't an abuser. It wasn't like my friend and other people I've seen who get so involved where they give up on their responsibilities.

Marijuana was something that he smoked like cigarettes. He was a very heavy smoker. He would carry the marijuana cigarettes in his wallet. My husband never said he had a problem of addiction, and I don't believe he had one, but he did carry marijuana cigarettes in his wallet. In fact, I recall that his breakfast was a marijuana cigarette, his lunch was a marijuana cigarette, and so was his dinner. He would do acid as well, but only occasionally.

I was opposed to his smoking. I tried making him stop by telling him that I was going to use it as well. But he would always say no, that I wasn't going to do it. Then I would tell him that he couldn't continue because he was harming himself. His response was that it was okay.

One thing about marijuana I really disliked was its smell. It had a terrible odor that I simply couldn't take. His friends would come in the house and smoke. My clothes and bedding smelled like marijuana, and I hated it. I was always spraying the house. My husband hated when I sprayed because it eliminated the smell or odor, and I suppose that the smell was part of the high and enjoyment. Because of this, there were constant arguments. Since we lived in a fairly large apartment, I would tell him to go smoke where I couldn't smell it. Or when he was smoking in the house with some friends I would go in the bedroom and slam the door as a symbol of my anger over what he was doing. This was my way of letting him know I didn't approve of his smoking. Then my husband, because he was high on drugs, would come to the bedroom door and say: "Lourdes, unlock the door. What's wrong with you? I'm not doing anything wrong. I'm just here with my friends." It was always that he was not doing anything wrong. At times he would come into the bedroom, and I would get upset because I knew that his friends knew what he was telling me, because they could hear him.

That was the most I could do. Eventually, my husband started going outside of the house and into the car for his smokes. So, I feel that he met me halfway. Since I always voiced my opinion about what he was doing, he came to realize that I was concerned. He didn't stop using, but at least he realized that I didn't want it in my house. Yet a new problem arose. Now that he was doing it outside, he started staying out longer and spending more time on the streets. So, there was no way to win.

Not only was Lourdes's husband a heavy drug user, he was also deeply involved in dealing drugs. He capitalized on their availability and the demand for drugs in his community during this period. He was one of many gang leaders who transformed the gang into a business enterprise. Lourdes's husband understood the benefits of using the gang as the cornerstone of his drug-dealing establishment: he could hire his own gang members on commission to sell at retail prices at the street level, with most of the profits going to him; his major responsibility was obtaining large amounts of drugs for distribution.

Like other young men at the time, my husband used the streets to make money. Money, through drug dealing, was made so easily and fast. He was one of those who was able to save money over time and get into the business later. He eventually became a true entrepreneur, with the exception that he was enterprising in drugs.

I wasn't blind to any of the things my husband was doing out in the streets. I suspected how some of the money he was bringing home was being generated. I just never gave it a second thought. Because there were lots of secrets—my husband always tried keeping things from me—I was left to know only a few items of information.

I didn't realize there was so much dealing going on until things started coming into the house. He started bringing pounds of the stuff [marijuana] into the house. He even brought a scale to weigh it. And when we would go grocery shopping he always bought small baggies to package the stuff. So, it became quite clear what he was up to. Whenever I tried talking to him about what he was doing he would say: "This is just the way it's gotta be. This is the only way to make money so we can be financially secure."

He wanted to make enough money to buy a house. He used to talk about buying a big house. According to my husband, the house needed to have at least three bedrooms, because we had to think of the children we were going to have. And he wanted a master bedroom with a nice bathroom. He wanted a nice and big kitchen. He also wanted a play area, where he was going to put a pool table and pinball machine. Finally, he wanted to make sure that the house had an extra bathroom for the guests; after all, he didn't want them using the same bathroom we used. These were his dreams.

Not for one moment did I give much thought to where the money was coming from to purchase this house. All that I could see was us together at all times. The house was going to be located in the suburbs, away from the city. I knew that it was not going to be easy to commute back and forth every day of the week.

He also wanted to start his own legitimate business. This was the dream: he wanted to use his gains to go legit. And he assumed all along that the gains were going to be plenty and that he was not going to spend it all. His plans were to open a store. I think what he had in mind was a grocery store. He also thought about opening up a restaurant.

What was I going to say to these plans? Although I was against what he was doing, I supported his ideas. I found myself having to show my support in order to maintain his high spirit. I thought that, if these things did happen, that he would then stop doing whatever he was doing out in the streets.

Drug dealing is, of course, filled with much danger and risk. For Lourdes this meant having to live under seriously stressful conditions; she worried constantly about her husband being arrested by the police or being shot by a member of an opposition gang. Lourdes also feared the possibility that the police would bust her house; she expected the police might break down her door at any time because her husband's activities were well known in the neighborhood.

When her husband was incarcerated for allegedly shooting and killing a member of another gang Lourdes took his place as distributor within the business. For her running the business was necessary because at the time it appeared to be the only way of earning the money needed to get her husband out of prison. With the profits she made Lourdes was able to pay the attorney's fees for her husband's first case and his subsequent appeal. Assuming the role of distributor, then, was a decision Lourdes agreed to entirely for her husband's benefit. Needless to say, her new role caused Lourdes even more stress and worry.

I was scared all the time because of what my husband was doing. One day I told him to tell me what was happening. Instead, he showed me how to package the stuff. I learned how to weigh a pound, an ounce, and how to bag the nickel and dime bags [common measures for packaging marijuana]. Though he was very private and always kept to himself, I believe it got to the point that he felt it was important for me to know what was happening in case something bad happened to him and he couldn't continue carrying out his role as a businessman. It was at this time that he decided:

"Okay, you want to know what I'm doing? This is exactly what's going on."

While he showed me the procedures for getting the drugs ready to be sold, I became very nervous, and this weird feeling came over me. I didn't like what was happening. He saw it as something that had to be done, so I just listened. I just knew that this wasn't for me. And, although I was so against what he was doing, I gave him more encouragement, always reminding him that things could be different. I guess he knew something was going to happen when he decided to show me the ins and outs of the business.

It wasn't until the time he was going out to make a deal and he was stopped by some detectives that were watching him that I fully learned the entire scope of what he was doing. It was only when this incident occurred that I learned that he was running this business, that he was making pickups and deliveries, that he was so involved. The detectives who got him insisted that he tell them where he was coming from, and when he refused they decided to take him away. But the landlord of the building where we lived, who was watching what was taking place from his apartment window, came up and ran to the door to tell me that my husband had just gotten arrested.

I thought, "Oh my God, what am I going to do?" I opened the door to one of our closets and found this huge box containing all kinds of drugs and guns. I immediately began thinking: "This is it—the police is gonna come, and I'm gone. They're going to put me away forever." I suspected his brothers knew what I needed to do. They were very close to my husband and to the business. So, I called them and asked them what to do. I was afraid to leave the house, but I was afraid to stay. They told me to just take it easy because nobody was going to come to the apartment. I told them that I was going to get out and take everything with me.

So, my husband's brothers agreed that I leave the apartment and told me that they would pick me up. I grabbed everything and put it in a laundry bag. Earlier in the day I had made plans to do my laundry, so I figured that I would put the stuff inside the laundry bag and cover it with the clothes. It really looked like I was going to do laundry. Since the police didn't know me, the worst they could have done was stop me and ask me to show them the clothes. When I came down to the street level I was terrified. Many thoughts crossed my mind. "I'm hoping that nobody is looking," was one persistent thought. I finally managed to compose myself.

I also took the money that was in the house and brought it along. We drove around for some time, to make sure nobody was following. We finally took everything to some place that I don't remember very well. But it was a close call.

I was scared of not only getting busted with all the stuff, but my fears had to do with the police coming into the apartment and breaking everything. I knew that, if they were issued a search warrant, they would come and ransack the apartment. I didn't want any of my property destroyed for something that was not my fault. We're lucky because we've never had our house broken into by the police.

After this incident my husband agreed not to leave anything in the house because I became hysterical. I told him that he needed to do something, that he couldn't keep his stuff in the house. Since he was doing well with the business, he decided to rent a different apartment, where he kept everything. The apartment that he rented was used solely for storage. It was not a rock house [a place where drugs are sold]; it was not something that was being used for selling. I made sure that the apartment did not have any furniture, like a bed. I went there unannounced several times, and it was bare.

When he was arrested and waiting trial for the case for which he was eventually sentenced to serve the seventy years, he said to me: "It's in your hands. You have to do this because I'm not coming home, and this is the only way you're going to pay the attorney who represented me in court. We're going to have an appeal, and we're going to need money for that too." My husband wanted me to continue running the business. His wish was for me to remain living comfortably. Although I knew this was all wrong, I agreed to do it. I went into the business and ran it for almost a year.

After he was sentenced I was numbed in terms of what was happening. So, when my husband asked me to run the business I accepted almost without any hesitation. I didn't even think straight. I was like a zombie; I would just get up in the morning and go to work, and then later it was time to return home. I didn't want to do anything but lay back and die. And when my husband told me to continue running his business I just said, "Fine." I didn't even care. My attitude was "I just don't care about anything." He could have told me to do anything, to jump from the moon, and I would have done it. Things simply didn't matter anymore at that point.

I ran the business without much difficulty, since I had learned its basic elements. I never had to buy merchandise; someone else did that job. My biggest responsibility was weighing everything, packaging and distributing it to the workers. Of course, I also collected the money.

There is no doubt that I was doing all of this for my husband. Nothing of what I was doing was for me. It was something that had to be done at that time. There was no other way around it. It was difficult to make decisions, and all I thought was that I had to get my husband out of prison, and, if that's what it was going to take, then that's what I was going to do.

The business was bringing in thousands of dollars, and we needed the money to pay for the attorney. The attorney had charged us over twelve thousand dollars to represent my husband in the initial trial. Then we had to pay him an additional seven thousand for the appeal case. How else was I going to raise that kind of money?

Drug dealing was also a way to raise cash to pay for the things I owed. I had credit cards that I used for putting gas in the car. I used the credit cards to purchase new clothes and groceries. I even took cash advances with them. I was literally using plastic to live. The cards were available; I went for them. That's the point in my life when everything was overwhelming and very confusing.

In the business I was playing the role of the distributor. I would get home from work at about 3:30 in the afternoon. I would go out to the street corner to talk to the guys who were dealing for me. I was there also to collect my money. Then I would go home, sit by the phone, and wait for people to call and tell me what they wanted. Running of the business would end about eleven or twelve. This was the routine.

No one was allowed to come up to my house. The only people who visited were those who ordinarily would come when my husband was home, those individuals he really trusted. They were like my brothers. I felt very safe with them. If other people wanted to talk to me, then we talked on the street. And my street interactions with people were always short, because I didn't want people to suspect me. I was really scared about running a drug-dealing operation. I used to dream of someone calling the cops and snitching on me. I was also very concerned about the way I would be viewed if people discovered what I was doing. I was quite aware how people in the neighborhood thought of women who were known for doing things like running a drug-dealing operation; they were perceived as being loose. I didn't want people to see me in that way because I wasn't a loose woman.

I hated what I was doing. It was simply not my character. I would see other people selling or carrying out an operation, and I would immediately think, "Don't they have a conscience?"

I just couldn't take running the business. The pressure was overwhelming. I couldn't sleep at night thinking about the possibility that someone would tell the police what was happening. I kept thinking that people were going to break in the door. I gave it up.

By now I was about nineteen years old. I had not returned to church. I don't know how I was able to endure all of this. Sometimes I wonder how I was able to take it. Maybe I was blinded by all the things that I thought I was receiving so easily. I think that when the poor get their hand on money they sometimes lose sense of themselves and of many other things. I feel that we get carried away with the sensation over the accumulation of so much wealth. Here I was doing whatever I wanted to in terms of being able to purchase things. I simply didn't give a second thought to what I was doing. It was very clear that I wasn't thinking very rationally.

The same people that worked for my husband were my workers. My husband simply told them that I was running things out there for a while and to give me respect. But there were problems from the moment that I moved in to run the business. In the world in which we lived then—and it's possible the same thing is happening today—it's very hard for a man to take orders from a woman. Although the guys that were working for me would listen, I couldn't deal with them the way my husband could; they did not take me seriously. They simply refused to accept that they were having to work for a woman. They devised different ways to make themselves feel like they had the upper hand.

For example, at times some guys would come and tell me that the cops busted them and everything was taken. What they were telling me was that they didn't have money to give me because their merchandise had been seized by the police. Since I was at work all day, I didn't know how truthful their stories were.

There was one particular individual who every time I asked him, "How much money did you make today?" he would say, "Oh, the police made a raid, and I lost everything I had." I could see this happening maybe once or twice but not five days out of seven. These guys were trained not to carry anything with them—they were trained to hide it—so I could not understand it. It was getting out of hand.

And this one day—I think I had had a hard day at work—he came up with the same story, and I began to think of doing something really bad to him. I developed a feeling for wanting to go home and get a gun that my husband had left me. For a brief moment I had wanted to shoot him—I was so upset.

I felt like I was being taken advantage of because I was a woman, and, because my husband wasn't there, they thought they could do whatever they felt like. Though they had every right to question my orders—nobody is subject to anyone else—they were involved in the business because they wanted to be. It's like having a regular employer: you either abide by the regulations the employer establishes, or you leave. So, if they wanted to continue working, they had to listen.

And in many cases it didn't function that way. These guys were pocketing the money. Since I'm no fool, I would become very angry, and a side of me was coming out that wasn't me. I was acting smug, like I didn't care about what I said or what I did. I didn't like myself very much. I didn't like the way I was thinking and acting. I just couldn't do it.

As the guys began making stories about how the cops were busting them and taking everything they had, I began to experience some heavy losses. Of course, what was happening to the business was that the money wasn't coming in like in the beginning. Because the money wasn't coming in, I wasn't balancing anything. In addition, there was very little money for reinvestment. Since I had these credit cards that I used for charging everything, I began to accumulate all kinds of debts.

It became obvious to me that this whole thing was wrong. It wasn't working out. I guess it wasn't supposed to be. A sense of individual consciousness of who I was was resurfacing. I was on my way to rediscovering my true identity because of all these problems with the business. I started to see the downturn of the business in a different way. Instead of concentrating on what was happening to the business, I began to pay attention to what was happening to me. I quickly realized that this person who was dealing in drugs, who was running a drug-dealing operation, wasn't me. And I was not going to stay doing this kind of work very long; I wasn't brought up this way. What I was doing wasn't honest. It wasn't my character.

Then there were two other major incidents that really brought me back to my feet and to my senses. If I needed an awakening, I got it from these two incidents.

The first involved my mother. One night my mother, who had keys to my apartment, came in through the rear door and discovered what I was up to. Since I knew that she could come in and out as she wanted, I was always very cautious not to let her find me doing any work that was affiliated with the drug-dealing business. But she knew all along what I was up to—she was my mother. Mothers know everything that their children do, even when the children try hiding it from them. And she walked in on me while I was bagging the merchandise to distribute to my workers. She actually busted me. She caught me with my hands in the cookie jar. I couldn't simply deny what I was up to; after all, she had caught me red-handed. I didn't know how she would react; I didn't know if she would throw it away, beat me—I didn't know.

To my surprise my mother didn't say one single word. She pulled up a chair, sat down next to me, and starting helping. It broke my heart. I realized that she knew what I was going through. I also thought that she knew what I had to do. What was wonderful about her reaction was that it did not judge me. She remained silent.

Finally, after a couple hours my mother spoke. Essentially, she told me about her worries and concerns for me: "We have to find another solution for this. I cannot take it if you get arrested or if someone comes into the house." "It's gonna kill me," she added. That was a bombshell.

After she left I cried. "What am I doing? What's happening with my life." I was so hurt. I didn't tell her anything for a couple of days. Then she visited and counseled me. She basically warned me about the danger of what I was doing. She repeated how she didn't want me to get hurt.

A day following my mother's surprise visit this little boy knocked on the door asking if he could deal for me. His brother was a dealer for my husband, so he knew about what we were doing. "I'll be good," said the little boy to me. That was the straw that broke the camel's back. I was so hurt. In the blink of an eye I saw that I was going to be responsible for the death of this young boy. I saw myself becoming responsible for his incarceration. In this little boy I saw an entire generation of children who were going to be ruined by people like myself. He represents a member of the next generation, the generation that we need to care for and nurture. Instead, we were going to contribute to its destruction. These were scary thoughts. I sent him home. I shouted to him: "Go home! This isn't for you." I couldn't take it.

I was dealing with so many emotions. I felt that I wasn't thinking straight. I was under an enormous amount of pressure. I felt that I had to do the things I did to survive. I was hoping that my husband was going to come home and all of the things I was doing would end soon. Then I discovered it wasn't going to happen exactly as I had planned, so everything changed completely.

It took these two incidents to set me straight. I finally came to see what I was doing. At this time the drugs and money were still in the house, and I wanted to get rid of it all. I wanted to destroy it all. I didn't want anything to do with the drugs or the money. I decided to put everything in a bag. Later I called one of the fellows and told him to take it and give me the money or do whatever. I just wanted to get rid of the stuff. At that point I was like, "I don't care if you come back with the money." I just wanted out. I wanted to live my life differently.

I felt great. I felt like I didn't owe nothing to nobody. I felt that, although it was going to be hard to make it on my own, I would no longer be responsible for anyone's death, incarceration, or overdose—this was a major concern of mine. I couldn't have dealt with the thought that this person died because of an overdose from the drugs he purchased from one of my workers. He could have bought it someplace else, but, still, the fact remained that I was selling the same stuff that took someone's life. That's why I see people today that are doing it, and I cannot understand how their conscience is not moved.

Later that night, when my husband called and learned what I had done, he said: "You can't do that. How are you going to make ends meet?" My husband was not upset over my decision to leave the business; he was just worried that I was not going to make it. He wanted to be sure that I was secure. I informed him that I refused to feel secure through drug dealing. I told him that I had a regular job, that I would live from the money I would earn at my job. I had made up my mind that I wasn't going to continue in this kind of business. I had decided that I wasn't going to live life like this anymore. I wasn't going to go crazy because of this. That's when I decided to look toward God.

God had always been there for me. I was so confused, so involved in everything that was happening, that I was not thinking straight. I realized that God was the only one that was gonna get me through, and I needed to find myself. I needed to look at life differently.

The business operation continued; the guys were running it. What was important was that I was out of the picture.

Not having that financial help come in to pay the rent and to pay the credit cards changed everything. Life wasn't easy. The bills started piling up like no other time before. I was used to charging things I bought, and when the bills came I had the money to pay, but not now. When my husband was first imprisoned I took the car he was using, which was already paid for, and traded it in for a new car. That was really crazy of me, but I thought that I was going to continue in the business. I thought I didn't have anything to worry about, but I did. Once I pulled myself out of the business I couldn't make the car payments; I couldn't pay the insurance on the car. I was barely making two hundred dollars a week. My husband would call every day to find out how I was doing. And, of course, things were the same. There were simply too many payments to make but not enough money. The situation was overwhelming for me to handle. Yet I was convinced that I would find some way for getting me out of all of this.

I started by selling our furniture as a way to raise some money. The only item that I kept was the bedroom set, because to me this was something that was very private, and it was the last thing my husband and I had together.

Later I decided to file for bankruptcy, something I never thought I would ever have to do. It was like everything that I had to work so hard for—things that I bought with my own money, my credit, the trust people had in me—everything was going down the drain. It was one of the most humiliating experiences I ever had. I knew that in time I would reestablish myself and purchase new things, but at that particular moment it was very hard and painful. It was a tough decision to make; it was something that brought a great deal of pain.

After the bankruptcy I left our apartment and went to live with the pastor of my church and his wife. They were fond of me. They only had one son, and I was like a daughter to them.

What really happened was that I went to stay with the pastor's wife for a weekend because her husband had gone to a convention, and her son was also gone, and she didn't want to be by herself. So, I said that I would stay with her for that weekend. That short stay became two years.

I also went to live with the pastor and his wife because I wanted some privacy and distance from my mother and my mother-in-law. I was afraid that, if I had gone to live with mother-in-law, it would had been the constant, "Oh, my son, my son, my brother, my brother." If I had gone home to my mother, she would have always said, "Oh, my daughter, you're suffering so much." I needed to go to a neutral place, where people would not choose sides. I also needed a place where I could stand on my own two feet without all the sorrow and pain.

My stay with the pastor and his wife produced a total change for me. They lived far enough from the neighborhood to enable me to have the space I needed to find myself. I didn't know how long my husband would be away, and I needed to start my life over again.

I began to regain my strength through the commitment the pastor and his wife have for God. I learned to rely on faith very, very much. Living with them enabled me to see how they dealt with their own personal problems and struggles. They didn't have a lot of money because we have a very small church, and we rely on the funds that come in from the church people. And, although they didn't have money, the pastor and his wife were still very content and happy. It wasn't like they would go up in an uproar if they didn't have something. They just took things one day at a time. If there was any money, it was fine; if there wasn't any, it was fine too.

They were not hysterical about their situation. I began to see the way they were and how they carried on their lives. In comparison, I was quite different. For example, I was one that would not eat rice and beans if there wasn't any meat to go along with that. There were many times that there wasn't any meat for the pastor and his wife to have with their rice and beans, yet there wasn't a big worry about that. They didn't have meat with their meal, but they had learned to manage. Their faith prevailed—the next day, perhaps, things would be different.

One major lesson I learned from them is that life does take its course, that what's going to happen happens, and you take it in stride and deal with it the best way you can. Sure, I might cry when hard times come; I might get upset and become depressed. But I just pick myself up again because I know that things are going to work out. From them I learned that you can't hide in yourself and say I can't do this and pity yourself.

4

Managing the Fact of Imprisonment

In his seminal work on stigma sociologist Erving Goffman uses the concept to refer to attributes and behaviors of individuals who, because of their unconventional activities, habits, and choices—such as alcoholism, drug addiction, mental illness, homosexuality, physical deformities, juvenile delinquency, and imprisonment—are dishonored and rejected by the larger society. According to Goffman, there are individuals with a "discredited stigma," those who assume that their differentness is already known about or is immediately evident, and individuals with a "discreditable stigma," those who assume that their stigma is neither known about by those present nor immediately perceivable by them (1963, 4). Goffman's work focuses on how people cope with these two forms of stigma.

Goffman's emphasis, however, is on the process whereby an intimate of the stigmatized person becomes "related through the social structure to the stigmatized individual, both being treated in some respects as one" (1963, 30). Goffman termed this procedure "stigma transference," or gaining "courtesy stigma." Sociologist Nancy Blum states that, although "not directly possessing *a stigma, the intimate becomes an insider to the stigma, so implicated in its everyday management as to be almost as vulnerable to discrediting" (1991, 264).*

A good part of Lourdes's married life has gone into coping with the stigma she incurred following her husband's imprisonment. For eight years Lourdes attempted to cope with her courtesy stigma by trying to pass as a normal person, trying to convey an image of conventionality.

As a stigmatized individual, Lourdes tried to control information to manage her "spoiled social identity," her identity as the wife of a drug user, gang leader, and prisoner. She was always careful in interactions and conversations that might reveal the stigma. Information she shared with others was presented, or packaged, so as to conceal the stigma and discourage further investigation. In conversations, when the topic of family would come up, she pulled away; she would change the subject quickly or simply end the discussion.

Lourdes had few close friendships. Several of the wives and mothers of other inmates were part of Lourdes's small circle of friends. She worked hard to keep herself at a distance from other people. If somebody tried to get too close, Lourdes withdrew from the emerging friendship. She even left several jobs because coworkers were beginning to ask about her husband's whereabouts.

With her family members Lourdes developed a protective circle, which helped to assure her that word about her husband's incarceration would not get out. Everyone worked together to live as normal lives as possible. For eight years Lourdes and her relatives did not disclose their "family secret."

These coping mechanisms led to moments of serious psychological stress for Lourdes. Her personal identity was affected intensely. She was living in near isolation; her social life was built essentially around her immediate family, church members, and her husband, who, of course, was not present. Further, it became cumbersome for Lourdes to keep neighbors and friends from knowing about her husband's imprisonment. She felt that she had to be alert at all times and, thus, was always on the defensive, prepared to take on any person who might try to trespass the lines of acceptable information.

Understanding then managing her life as a person with a stigma began for Lourdes with coming to terms with her actual conditions: "How do I face the world as the wife of a prisoner? What am I supposed to say to people? Is it worth living when everyone seems to be judging and treating me like a criminal?" Managing her particular stigma was made more difficult for Lourdes when she decided to become involved in helping her husband deal with his own situation as an inmate. He had become preoccupied with his identity as a prisoner and Lourdes's as the wife of a prisoner, and his way of thinking was wreaking havoc on him emotionally. Because of her husband's difficulties coping, life was unpredictable, and it was extremely difficult for Lourdes to establish a routine that would allow her to deal with her own discomfort at being labeled the wife of a prisoner. She realized then the importance of helping her husband to become more cooperative and understanding of her needs as well as his own—of working together to handle their separate yet related circumstances.

During the time I was working the business, I was still hopeful that my husband was coming home. We were waiting for the trial, and I was convinced that justice would prevail and he would be let go, but it did not happen that way. I came to realize that I was going to have to live without him. I finally realized that our married life was going to have to be carried out with him inside the prison walls and with me on the outside.

"How do you live such a life?" I asked myself this question a thousand times, but, of course, this was a new experience for me. I did not know what to do or say to people. Under these circumstances people often say that you're not alone, that you still have your family. But I could have been surrounded by millions of people, and I still felt alone. In fact, that's exactly how everything was. I was among many, many individuals, yet I found myself with no one.

The first couple of years were the worst. I was under a great deal of stress and depression. There was no sense going on with life under these terms. It was very hard to go on living; I wanted my life to end. I even contemplated suicide. I would go to work in the morning and look at the train coming and think, "Should I, or shouldn't I?" But then I would think of my mother and think that I could not do this to her. Why should she suffer also? She did not deserve it; she had nothing to do with what happened to me.

The idea of committing suicide carried some strange feelings. I was brought up believing the Bible: life was given by God, and only God has the authority to take it. Here I was contemplating suicide when I knew that it was wrong. I knew what the outcome of suicide was. I knew that if I committed suicide, I wasn't going to heaven— that thought was fresh in mind. I understood very well that I wanted to go to heaven, but at the same time I was fighting with the feeling and emotions of knowing that my husband had left me out here to struggle on my own. I was blaming him for the way I was feeling.

I was so hurt that I wanted him to hurt. I wanted him to be in such pain, like when you're bent over with pain because you can't take it. That's exactly how I felt. No amount of counseling or support from anybody was going to take away the pain I felt. This pain that I was feeling inside was destroying me, and I wanted him to hurt the same way. I wanted him to realize how deeply hurt I felt.

My husband was also frustrated. I would go visit him, and he would be like: "So, what happened? Where did you go? What did you do?" I think that he was afraid that I would leave him, that I would take off with someone else. This is usually what goes through the minds of these guys once they are in the inside. They have seen so many cases of wives and girlfriends who left as soon as the incarceration occurred. Also there were other inmates telling him: "Well, my wife left me. And you come in here with seventy years, do you think she's gonna wait?" But this did not apply to me. I would tell him that I was at church; I would go there to cry. I used to tell my husband that I was going to wait, not to concern himself with me. His overprotection of me also caused him to be so alarmed; he couldn't protect or shield me from where he was, and that really upset him.

It was a very stressful time. I wanted God to take me. I wanted Him to end it right there. I didn't want to go on living anymore. Since God refused to take me every time I asked Him, I just prayed and put my faith in Him.

Although I didn't know it at that time, my husband felt hurt and alone. When we were together in the outside he had relied on me as much as I relied on him. And when I could no longer be by his side he felt like his life was over. At first I didn't realize how he really felt because he would not share his feelings with me. And, since he was surrounded by his friends in prison, I used to think that, since his friends were there, everything was normal for him. I used to think that for him it was business as usual, but I was wrong.

On New Year's Eve—I think it was in 1982—I was in church praying and asking God to do something: "You have to take control of his life; you have to take control of his way of being somehow because I cannot continue like this. I'm gonna go crazy." The next day my husband called me, and I found him to be different. He told me that at twelve o'clock on New Year's Eve he got on his knees and started to cry because he realized everything that had happened. On this particular day, when he was on his knees crying, he picked up a Bible that I had sent to him along with other literature, and he read from it. He said that he felt comfort, some type of relief, from reading it. I always told him to read and to try to find comfort in the Bible. I think that he was given some strength by God.

From this point on he knew he had to change. He began to accept the fact that the only way that he was going to make it was by being more determined. He also told me that he knew that nothing was going to break us unless we want it to. So, from that moment on we relied on each other more and more.

It was good to hear him sound optimistic, but I still had mixed feelings. I felt relieved because he was beginning to adjust to his situation, but you can't ever adjust to a situation like that. I knew that things were going to be very difficult for him, even though he was changing and turning to God in order to deal with his struggle.

As my husband calmed down and started expressing himself to me, communicating and sharing things, it became easier to deal with my own situation. I felt like I was breathing again. I was able to go here and there and not have to worry because I knew that he felt really confident.

Still, there were many times when I wanted to give up. I don't mean giving up on him in the sense of leaving him. It's just that I couldn't live with being on my own. You have to grow up and realize that you have to do things by yourself. When we were first married I was very dependent on him. I worked, but he took care of everything else.

I woke up one day, and the world was staring at me. The world was looking directly at me and challenging me to take it on. I realized I needed to do things I never did before. If I refused, I was going to be easily defeated—it was that simple. So, I learned how to take care of a lot of things. A good example is this morning when I had to get the car to go on. I got up, I got ready for work, and when I went downstairs to start the car it didn't want to go. So, I lifted the hood and knew exactly what was wrong. As a wife alone, I had to learn how to take care of everything. I have become the man and the woman of the home. But, again, at first this was difficult because my husband had made me very dependent on him.

It's all his fault: we had our ups and downs, but he tended to spoil me. Even to this day his family says that he spoiled me too much. I guess they are right. He would pick me up from work, take me out to eat and then to the show. He was very spontaneous, and he would always do things like that. There were times when he would stop at a store, and, if he saw something nice, he would not look at the price and buy it for me.

I have this big stuffed rabbit that he bought me once because he thought I would like it. He gave it to me on Easter. I was coming home from work, and he was standing on the corner with his friends when he called me over. And I said, "Yeah, what is it?" He told me to open the trunk of his car because there was something he had bought for me. When I opened the trunk this big rabbit popped out. And all the guys who were standing there were like, "Ohh." It made me feel real special because I didn't really see that from his other friends. It takes a lot of heart and love to do something so touching like that. And, so, I was walking down the street toward home with my rabbit, and I could see the glow on his face. He felt like he had given me a million dollars.

There are many other stuffed animals around the house that everyone who visits can see. Then there are many others that I have in one bedroom where my niece sleeps. These are very meaningful things, because of the satisfaction I had of knowing that he was giving them to me because he cared. That was part of the way he spoiled me. He made sure that my emotional needs were met. I think that he felt good to be going out of his way to do something nice for his wife. He would always tell his friends how important it was to be good to a wife. He would tell them not to hurt her by fooling around and making her suffer; his suggestion was to always treat her good. And I really believe that he tried being and doing all those things.

It felt great to be spoiled. What can I possibly say? I can't say I didn't like being spoiled by my husband. In fact, I have not met a person who does not enjoy being spoiled. It's a good feeling. It tells you how concerned that other person is. It shows that other person's love for you. There are different ways of spoiling people. A person can be spoiled and turn out rotten. Another person could become good.

My husband wasn't out to make me a handicapped person. I don't really think that he was doing these things to control me and make me dependent on him. He wasn't spoiling me to take advantage of me—I don't think so. He knew how I was. He cared and this was his way of showing his love for me. He was a husband who cared about my feelings and who wanted to make sure that I was feeling good.

If my husband spoiled me, I spoiled him just as much. He was very dependent on me as well. Since I was working, I always used part of my money to buy him things, in particular clothes. I loved to buy him clothes—that is one thing I really enjoyed. He never went out shopping for himself. He depended on me. He wasn't picky like I've seen guys in some families who, after someone buys them clothes, they say, "I don't like that shirt you bought me; I don't like those pants." My husband was always very grateful and proud to wear what I bought for him. Besides, I always had good taste.

To buy him clothes and seeing him wearing them also said that he was mine. It said that I was the only one who could do that; that was my protection. Was I protective? Without any doubt. I was his wife, and he was my husband. Wives are supposed to be protective of their husbands.

So, at that time I didn't resent being so dependent on him. I felt that the dependency was a two-way street. Maybe there should be more of this type of husband and wife interdependency. I would not call it dependency; rather, it has to do with relying on one another and sharing and caring. People today are growing more and more apart from one another: the wife does this with "her money," and the husband goes here and buys this or that with "his money." I think that's a terrible way of life. This is like living two separate lives. People don't have much to do with one another. If a person agrees to get married, that person should commit to giving and taking. That's exactly what we did.

On the other hand, I did feel resentful once he was gone and away from me for good. I resented the fact that, while I was so dependent on him, he was not dependent on me. Yesterday we were talking on the phone and reminiscing about times that we spent together out here in the world. I was telling him that he never told me how he relied on me for certain things. He did not agree. He said that during one time, when I took a trip to Puerto Rico with my mother and he couldn't come because he was too busy out on the streets, that he missed me very much. He said that he missed not having me around him. I said, "You never told me you missed me."

I think the reason why he did not tell me how he felt before was that his machismo did not allow him. There is the stereotype of the Latino man who is not supposed to hurt, feel pain, or be expressive. The woman is the only one who is supposed to be weak, and she is the one who is supposed to express herself openly. When she is in pain she cries; when she suffers an injury she openly reveals the pain to others. Guys in our culture are brought up to think this way. There is a very specific form of behavior for them to adapt to, and it doesn't include opening up and sharing their feelings with others. They are raised not to be expressive. They could be dying and would not speak out or show the pain they are suffering. So, perhaps that prevented him from opening up to me. Now that he is in prison and after making major adjustments in his life, he tells me about how he really felt and the changes that he went through. There was a great deal of pain and hurt inside of him. But, since he never actually told me, I didn't know what his real feelings were.

Our situation now is quite different; the shoe is on the other foot. I have become stronger and very independent. Sometimes I still rely on him for things, but I've become so that I can see myself living alone for the rest of my life if I have to and handle it and not fall apart like in the beginning—but who really knows?

The self-sufficiency Lourdes believes she gained was slow to develop. It took her a long time to arrive at the point of doing things for herself. Accepting her huband's status as a prisoner was in itself a slow process. Lourdes knew quite well that society's reaction to prisoners and their relatives was rarely favorable; she understood that both are stigmatized and often treated with fear and disdain. Lourdes had to learn to adapt to this new situation.

Becoming independent in terms of learning to do things I had not done before was difficult, but not as difficult as facing up to the reality that my husband was imprisoned. He was "serving time"— that phrase had such an ugly ring to it at first. I was going to have to deal with the fact that in our society a prisoner is defined as the worst of all imaginable elements. A prisoner comes to represent the scum of the earth. Everyone is of the opinion that a person is in prison because he did something very terrible. In fact, I think that most people feel that prisoners should all be killed or at least kept in prison until they die.

Then the mother, or the wife, is treated in criminal-like ways. People think that, if your husband is in prison, you must be a criminal too. In my situation I responded to it in different ways. Some individuals who got to know me over time, their evaluation of me was that I was a fairly nice person. But the minute they would find out that my husband was incarcerated, this light would go off over their heads, and they begin to think: "Hm, I wonder why. Could she be like him?" We are made to feel like we have committed a crime. Over the years I have reached the conclusion that women like me are truly prisoners in the eyes of the society. So, what happened to me was that, because of this view that I believed people had of me, it did not matter what I did or said, their view was fixed in their heads. To them I was a prisoner; to them I had committed a crime.

Members of Lourdes's family as well as those of her husband's became closer as they rallied together to keep others from learning about what had happened to Lourdes's husband. The families believed that, to maintain the dignity of all of those implicated, it was best to conceal information. For Lourdes denial became a way of life and the best way of dealing with society's stigmatization of her husband-prisoner. By not allowing anyone to know about her husband's incarceration, Lourdes found a survival strategy for living from day to day. For eight years Lourdes held people at a distance, making sure that what she said and did would not serve as clues to her actual world.

Of course, living a life of secrecy and denial was extremely difficult. It was a way of life filled with great emotional stress and with personal changes that were highly risky to Lourdes.

I didn't want anyone to know that my husband was in prison. For almost eight years I didn't want to talk about what had happened to my husband. I worked very hard to keep his incarceration a secret, not because I was ashamed; I just wanted to be protective of my feelings and his. I didn't want anyone to judge him or me.

For the most part my main coping mechanism was to remain very quiet at all times. Unless I told people, no one knew that my husband was incarcerated. I didn't have many friends other than the ones I came in contact with at the prison. Not having too many friends helped a lot. I never allowed people to become too friendly or close. I didn't want them to begin inviting me to their parties. I didn't want people asking me to host a get-together at my house. There were a few who did get close to me, and when they tried to figure out why my husband wasn't around during the Christmas parties, or if the subject would come up as to his whereabouts, I would just say: "He can't come. He's busy working."

Then, on other occasions, when my workmates would start asking too many questions, I simply changed jobs. Over the past seven years I've changed jobs three or four times because people were getting too close to my personal life, and I didn't want them to know.

To change from one job to another like I did was risky. I didn't know if I was going to be able to find another. It was also very frustrating because each time I was having to start all over again. I had to go through this thing of ensuring that people saw me as just another regular person.

It seemed like I was living a double life. I was working and trying to fit with my coworkers, who always talked about family relationships, about going home to cook because their husband was coming home at such and such a time. They were always talking about planning for the holidays, and I tried to fit in the conversation, pretending that everything was normal. This was difficult because, in actuality, I was coming home to an empty house.

There were many times that, as soon as I walked in through the door of my house, I would just cry. I was so frustrated. I was sick and tired of not being able to discuss how I really felt. It was really getting to me. There were times when, while talking to my husband, he would ask me, "What's wrong?" and I would snap at him. I wanted to tell him about the things I was having to go through in order to prevent people from knowing about him, but I didn't. I think I was afraid that he was going to misunderstand me. I was afraid that he was going to say, "Well, why don't you tell people?" or "Are you ashamed of me?" My husband didn't know how I had to cope with his imprisonment at work. So, I had all of this bottled up inside. I felt that I couldn't talk to anybody.

That was the double life I was living. I had to come home and be frustrated and cry, then wake up the next day, go to work, and make it appear like everything was just fine. Each day was exactly the same. And each day I was more frustrated with my situation.

But the most difficult part was trying to keep my family from Puerto Rico from finding out. My relatives who lived in Chicago knew what had happened, and they became very supportive. The ones in Puerto Rico did not know, and I tried hiding it from them. I don't know if it was a case of feeling embarrassed or not. All I know is that I didn't want them to know. I felt like I was the only one in the family who had someone who was incarcerated and serving time in a prison. I used to think that I was the only one to tarnish the character and image of the family. How could I have done such a thing to a family with so much dignity? I couldn't face up to what had occurred. I felt embarrassed that it was my fault because I had married a gang member. All of my cousins were quite successful and had successful families. They did not bring problems to the family; I did. These thoughts prevailed in my mind for a long time.

So, I wanted to hide the fact that my husband was in prison from my relatives who were away and did not know. I wanted them to think that I was fine, that my marriage was fine. But, in fact, I was guarding my feelings and trying to protect the reputation of the family.

There is the case of my grandmother, who died five years ago, not knowing that my husband had been incarcerated. Grandparents are considered the elders, or the wisest and most knowledgeable element of our family. We were brought up to give them respect, honor, and love. So, I refused to tell my grandmother, and I did not allow anyone to tell her.

My grandmother had met my husband when we first got married. One time when she came from Puerto Rico to spend some time with my mother, and my husband was already serving his sentence, I made sure to be the one to visit them. I didn't let them come over to my house because they were going to find only me there. And when I did go for a visit to see my grandmother I didn't spend much time with her. She would ask me about my husband, and I would just tell her that he was working a lot and not to worry that he would come and see her before she returned to Puerto Rico. He never did. I don't know if she suspected anything, but no one ever told her anything. I think that, if she suspected anything, it was probably that we were separated, and I didn't want to tell her that. I don't think she would have imagined that he was incarcerated.

The same thing almost happened with my grandfather. He would come from Puerto Rico to visit us and never see my husband. Keeping him from knowing that my husband was incarcerated hurt me so much. I was in pain. But by this time I didn't want to hide the truth any longer. There was a part of me that wanted to tell him, but there was another part of me that said no. I didn't want to hear or feel that he was disappointed about the person I had chosen for a husband. I didn't want him to feel sorry for what I was going through. There was a lot of mixed feelings that I didn't know how to deal with.

The hurt was so deep that on his last visit I told my aunt to please tell him what had happened. I couldn't face up to him. She told him. She was very sensitive to my feelings; apparently, my aunt painted a very nice picture of what had happened. My grandfather had always babied me, and, after discovering what had happened to my husband, he was even more compassionate.

He did it in such a loving way. It was really something. I will never forget that moment. He was at my aunt's house, and I went to visit him, and my aunt told me, "He already knows." I went up to him and gave him a kiss, and he just hugged me and kissed me and never said anything else. He never mentioned it or questioned it. It was like this thing was not happening—that meant a lot to me.

It felt good because I didn't want to talk about it, but, if he had questioned me, I was ready to answer. But he didn't. He saw what I was going through and decided not to even bring it up.

A return to the Pentecostal church became the most successful coping mechanism for Lourdes. The solution to her difficult situation was, she felt, to be found in the most basic of all social institutions: the church. Because of all that had happened in her life, Lourdes's vision had become clouded, and for years she discounted the important role the Pentecostal church had played in her early years. In time she remembered, and it was natural for her to come back to the church.

My husband's imprisonment came into my life as a bombshell. The only person I had to turn to was God because I know that He's always there, although it took a while before I turned to Him. I turned all my strengths upon Him, and I'm glad that I finally did. There are times when, as a human being, I get sad; I get very lonely, especially during the holidays. My situation is very hard, but I always try to carry my chin up like everything is fine, even though inside I'm dying.

Religion has helped me enormously in this ordeal. It was not difficult to seek emotional and spiritual relief and support from the church since my roots are Pentecostal. It took a while to return to my roots because, psychologically, I was confused. Many of us make mistakes in life, and at times it takes some of us time and different experiences to finally recognize what we are doing with our lives. But, after turning around, and it took a while to do that because it seemed that the corner was very long and wide, I learned that you can get strength from God in a very special way. Going back to church after all of this had happened, after spending time running my husband's business, I realized that something was there to provide me with what I really needed to heal.

The Pentecostal fundamentals are the same as in other faiths: believing, trusting, having confidence, having love for one another, and not hating. Hate causes more pain, and that was a lot of what I had. I was carrying an enormous amount of hate, and it was causing me a great deal of confusion and pain. So, after getting rid of those negative feelings, it was easier to cope with my situation from the point of view of the person that I was. Getting rid of the hate made me feel much better as a person because I came to realize that, above all, there is God. And trusting in someone that I couldn't see nor touch makes everything else kind of fit because that's what faith is all about. Faith is believing in what a person can't see. Faith is trusting what you still don't know—and that helped me to cope with a lot of things.

It's like the story of Noah and the Ark. This is the story about the time when God promised that He would never destroy the earth again with a storm. Storms are supposed to be natural and persistent parts of the physical world. The story tells us that into our lives a lot of storms come, but after they are all gone we expect a rainbow. That's the significance of the rainbow. It stands for the celebration of life after the storm. This belief is what keeps me going. So, although it's very cloudy, very stormy right now, eventually the rainbow must shine directly on my life. That convinction, the faith that my present life cannot be it—believing in yourself and in others, believing that it's not all pain and hate, that there is good—all of these things combined, which to me actually represent one mass, keep me going. One must find good in everything one does.

The Pentecostal church teaches you that there is a God as well as a supreme being of darkness, I don't want to call it a "supreme being," but there is the opposite side. It's like a defense attorney and a prosecuting attorney. There is a struggle between the two, and only one will win. The *right* side should win. You have a soul to gain or to lose. This body that we all have is going to stay here; it's going to be put in the ground; it's going to be eaten up by the worms, or whatever; it's going to be ashes to ashes, dust to dust. But we have a spirit that eventually will go someplace. It's now in life that you choose where it's gonna go. It's not after death, because, if it was like that, in vain, what was the significance of Jesus Christ dying on the cross? The point is that we choose the directions of our life. God has given us the wisdom to tell the right from the wrong; we can see that. For example, drugs are harming our bodies—we can see that—so why do drugs? It's just that at some points in our lives we're blinded by the glamour and bright lights of the other side.

I was there before. I felt hurt and hate. But I finally turned around and found God. From that moment on I turned more and more to Him. Many times I would go home and pray and talk to Him. Praying and talking aloud to Him is part of my religious practice. That's how I do it. I talk to Him as an individual. I'm sure that, if someone was to walk into my house when I'm praying to Him, talking to Him, that person would think that I was losing it, but this is how I feel this special closeness.

Although I don't get a verbal response from Him, I feel a satisfaction knowing that I'm able to let it all out. On these occasions I'm able to release my pain, my anger, my frustration, whatever feeling I'm experiencing; I can do this by talking out loud, because somehow, some way, I feel He understands what I'm going through. And many times I feel a closeness because I feel that God is just right there, catching all my tears and telling me that everything is going to be alright.

I now know I'm not alone in this, that I have this special power with me that gives me the courage to go on. That special power comes from God and the Holy Spirit. And it's just so hard to describe, but it's the closeness that you cannot have with anyone else. He is your best friend, the person who will hear you and not be judgmental, like we are at times. He won't reproach you; that's the fulfillment I've had. Like, if I went to a coworker and told her that I was having trouble handling the fact that my husband was incarcerated, she would say, "You're crazy; walk away." And, so, with Him I don't have to deal with that. I can just go home and meditate and feel so much better and not have to worry that someone would tell me how to feel.

By praying, I have developed a confidence that He is hearing me. I realize that He is not in my presence physically, but through the Holy Spirit I have that assurance that He is listening. It is difficult to explain, but there are many times when I'm really down, and I go into my room, and before I have kneeled down completely I just start to pray and feel different and better. It's like all of a sudden I feel so relaxed. I feel so good. I feel like I let it all out.

I don't want to make it sound like I have some kind of magical powers that no one else can see or understand. What I'm saying is that this inner strength that God gives, the sense of knowing that you're not alone, is something that I feel, and it's something that has become one of my ways for dealing and coping with my situation. The best way I can describe it is to compare it to the poem "Footprints," the poem about footprints in the sand by the unknown author. According to the poem, this man is feeling so good because all the scenes of his life were flashing in front of him, and he saw these sets of footprints, his and God's. He saw that God was always next to him. Then there was a time in life when things became very difficult, and he questioned God about it. He said, "When I needed you the most you leave me." And that's when God answered: "I never left you; I've always been with you. It is just that during times of suffering, in your most difficult times, you can only see one set of footprints, when in fact that's when I carried you." And that's the way I feel sometimes. I feel like He's carrying me when I just can't walk anymore.

When I returned to church the people there were very supportive. Their support helped me emotionally to cope. They knew what had happened with me. They suspected what I was going through, but we didn't talk very much about it. At first, when people did find out, they were shocked. They couldn't believe that something like that could happen to someone like me. But they accepted my condition and tried to give me love and care.

When you're a member of the church it's like one whole body. We cry together. We laugh together. When someone is hurting we all hurt. The best way to deal with pain and hurt is to just pray. I can put my hand across someone who I know is suffering from pain, but the best thing I can do for the person is to pray. There are times when you can talk to a person, but there are times when only praying is the best medicine.

This is so because sometimes words are not enough. And, dealing with what I was dealing with and still am, that was all I wanted. I wanted to walk into church and have someone just hug me and not tell me anything.

I was hugged many times, even to this day. There are many loving people in our church; they are always very concerned. It's like they are always cheering me on. It's like they are always saying: "Lourdes, yes, we are with you. How is your husband doing?" Most do not even know my husband, yet they send him best wishes every time they see me. It's a good feeling.

There is one woman in our church—she is not what you would call an old woman, but she is up in age—and she is a dear lady. She walks into church and comes to me to give me these big hugs. She then asks me, "How are you doing, and how is your husband?" She is always asking me about him, yet she has never met him. Then she tells me: "Oh, I'm praying for him. I know God is going to do something great because you are just so wonderful. And I can see how God is just using you because I'm able to." On other occasions, when I have given a talk at church, immediately after I finish she comes over to me to say: "Oh, you're such a blessing. God is using you. Everything is going to turn out good. Don't you worry." Her comments and support make me feel so great and wonderful.

On one particular occasion I was preaching about the book of Job, and this wonderful lady became ecstatic after I finished. The title of the story I was reading from is "¿Por qué sufre el justo?" (Why Does the Just Man Suffer?). It is about a man who is very close to God and would make sacrifices just in case his children have sinned on those occasions when they went out to parties. He wanted them to be saved. Satan decided one day to talk to God. God said: "Did you see my son Job? He is great, isn't he?" Satan answered: "That's because he has everything. If you take away his things, watch how he is going to curse you." The story goes on to say how God told him, "I'm going to permit you to destroy everything he has, but don't touch his soul." To make the story short: he lost his family; he lost a big amount of the cattle he had. Even his body was affected. It got to the point where his wife told him, "Why don't you curse God?" Instead, he continued to believe that God was faithful, that God was Judge. At the end he was given everything in twice the amount: he had a much bigger family; his daughters were recognized as the most beautiful daughters of all the land; all of his riches were multiplied.

The point is that, although we have trials and tribulations, there are going to be things that we will not understand. But, as long as we have faith, even if our faith is as big as a mustard seed, we can tell the mountain to move, and it's going to move. All God requires from us is to have faith.

My experiences have been hard, but I always use them when speaking in church because I have faith that the storm is going to pass and the sun is going to shine.

This particular day in church I kept on reading, and this woman came up to me and said: "Oh, I can always feel you; you're so positive. Watch, your husband is going to be back with you. God has always done great things." This woman is such a tower of strength. There are times when I get upset because something goes wrong in church, and I've responded by threatening to quit. But she always catches up with me when she notices that something is wrong. She says: "You're here to serve God and not man. You don't walk away like that; you have to keep on going."

Lourdes decided that returning to school to complete her high school degree was of utmost importance. After accomplishing this goal, Lourdes continued to attend school, receiving college credits to improve her job opportunities.

Though Lourdes benefitted enormously from school, its actual function was to serve as another coping strategy.

In addition to church involvement I started attending school. I decided to return to school. I started by taking courses to earn the general education diploma (G.E.D.). I did that easily. I became a high school graduate, or, at least, I had the equivalence of a high school diploma. After that any time there was a new course in school I would get in it. I took some courses at Truman College; I took courses at the Institute for Financial Learning. Through my job I went to a lot of seminars at different colleges, but it was for a brief time.

Although to this day I have a special feeling for school, I became involved in school because this was another way to keep my mind on something else besides my own reality. School kept me busy and away from people who might have wanted to know the whereabouts of my husband. Since Truman College was located far away from my neighborhood, I did not expect to meet anyone there who knew me. The location was safe.

Attending school was important because it helped me to keep my mind occupied with academic work. I was coming home to do homework and school assignments, rather than to think of what I was going through with my husband. My brother thought that I was going to go crazy because I was involved in so many things. But I always told him that I needed to do all those things in order to cope. There were times when I was very tired, yet I still studied for my classes or for exams.

Dealing with her situation was made easier when Lourdes decided to stop blaming her husband for the pain and suffering she was experiencing and, instead, became convinced that the situation could improve if she served as his support system and he as hers. Things had turned around completely for

Lourdes; whereas before he had been the one to accept responsibility and try to keep his wife calm and secure, now it was Lourdes's husband who needed her assistance in dealing with his imprisonment. Knowing that her husband was relying on her was for Lourdes a form of gaining power.

For a long time I felt like I was the only wife who had a husband incarcerated. I was feeling that I was the only one going through something like this. But there were many more people than just me who were suffering from the same predicament. I came to realize that I simply couldn't continue hiding and avoiding meeting and talking with people. I was living my life on guard, making sure that no one found out. It was important that I find specific ways that could allow me to be myself.

One of the things I did was to stop blaming him. Like many other women, I used to blame my husband for creating these conditions for me. I used to think: "He did this to me. Now I'm here by myself." Instead, I accepted the fact that, no matter how angry I was, I was the only support he had. But how was I going to help him if I was always blaming him? I needed to think of our situation in a different way. I realized that I could blame him for the rest of my life and not get anything out it. Blaming him made me bitter and angry. I was a very unhappy person, and I did not want to live my life that way. So, I decided to finally come to terms with what happened and go forward.

When you become your husband's system of support what that does in essence is to turn things around. The woman is now the one with the power. When married and living together in the outside world many women are abused by their husbands. Some are controlled; others cannot say yes or no to things that are happening in their lives. In the new situation the roles are reversed. She doesn't really need him; he needs her. She has the upper hand. He needs her support like no other time before. The woman gives her husband the support he needs to make it in prison; at the same time she benefits because she has gained the kind of power she never had before.

So with imprisonment the marriage begins to balance out. There is more equity. The husband is not the sole ruler, dictating to the woman, telling her what to do and how to do it.

There is more give and take. Take, for example, myself. I was very dependent on him. I used to listen to a lot of the things he said to me. Now I say, "You have to listen to me," and most of the time he responds by saying, "You're different now." And I say: "No, you made me grow up. You made me who I am now. You left me out there to grow up, and that's what I did. I'm a person—my own person."

I think that my husband thought of me as this young girl with no children and no responsibilities and who could have done whatever she wanted. At one point, before he was even sentenced, he talked to me about divorce, and I became very angry. I said: "You want to be so proud and make the decisions yourself. You want to be able to say, 'Well, I left her; she didn't leave me.'" I told him he wasn't going to get out of it that easily. I thought he was making the decision for both of us, and I felt insulted by that because, if a decision to leave or divorce was to be made, I was going to be the one to make it. If anything, the decision should be up to me, and I have made the decision to stick it out. I told him, "You should give me the respect to say, 'Okay, we are going to work this out.'" After this he never brought up the topic. He wanted to have the last word, and I didn't let him get away with it.

Of course, I made mistakes trying to make things work by myself, but that comes with the territory. I learned an enormous amount from the mistakes I made. But I was responsible for correcting my own mistakes; I was truly becoming a person responsible for her own actions.

This sounds like a terrible way to become empowered, but it worked out that way. Women become empowered through different events and experiences. For me it was through my husband's imprisonment.

With the more power I gained I was certain that we were going to be together forever. On top of that my convictions and principles from how I was raised, "until death do you part," meant I was going to remain married to my husband. Simply because he's out of my home doesn't mean I should leave him. He's just not there, but he's my husband; he's alive. Because of that, I've always said that I got to stick to it. Moreover, it's the love I feel for him.

I didn't like the way our marriage was being carried on then or now. It has been difficult for many reasons. Take, for example, those days when I come home from work tired and frustrated over something that happened during the workday. I don't have anyone at home to talk with about this. If something is bothering me on Monday, and I want to tell my husband, I have to wait until Saturday. By then the problem has gone away; there is nothing to tell him. I need to tell him at that very precise moment when I'm experiencing the problem. Not having that person there, not being able to pick up the phone and say, "This is what happened today," makes our marriage extremely difficult.

I want my husband out here, in the world, with me and his family, but that might not happen for a while. So, in the meantime we must continue living as a married couple.

But I also needed to accept that our marriage was going to be different. I knew quite well that we needed to develop a new form of marriage because he was inside, while I was outside. We had to figure out a way of keeping our marriage going. What we needed to do was find ways to keep each other going even though we were apart; we learned that we could exist even though we see each other once a week. The time that we would spend together was going to be very special. There were not going to be any fights.

Agreeing to this kind of marriage was going to help me to cope. I didn't have to worry so much about the fact that we were separated.

This is how things were going to be, and, regardless how much or little I cried, he was going to remain inside and apart from me.

Along with this came the realization that I needed to take each day at a time. I realized that I couldn't think of his sentence in terms of seventy years. I couldn't continue saying that. I discovered that, by saying "One more day, just one more day," it was much easier. For example, I've made it a habit to always celebrate the New Year at church. We pray at church on this day. I say to God: "It didn't happen this year, then maybe next year. Just give me the strength to take one day at a time."

I thank God that I get to wake up in the mornings. I thank God that I'm able to close out the day. Then I pray that the next day will be better. And, if it isn't, then I ask him to give me the strength and wisdom toward higher things. Sometimes everything in a day goes well, yet I want to scream at the top of my lungs: "But why not yet? Why haven't you answered? Why isn't this nightmare over? Why can't I live my life in a normal way now? When is it going to happen?"

For Lourdes work offered another way of coping. Working with people who are severely ill or handicapped has provided Lourdes with a new way of considering her situation as a prisoner's wife and how it resembles or is different from others. Within this expanded context she does not see herself as disadvantaged. In fact, when she compares her situation with the difficult lives of those individuals and families she works with, Lourdes feels very fortunate indeed.

Another thing that has helped me deal with my situation involves my work. I'm presently the supervisor of a program that serves the handicapped and people up to the age of fifty-nine who are experiencing serious sicknesses. We are serving people from different ages. We can serve a child today, tomorrow a senior, and the next day a teenager. We have all three generations in the program, which means that I get to see different hardships and the different ways people use for dealing with their conditions.

It becomes stressful when you have to work with a member of a family, knowing that you can't serve her because she may have a serious personal problem or sickness. I have visited many families and have seen a mother trying to deal with a son who was diagnozed as HIV-positive. I have seen a mother trying to deal with a baby that was born with AIDS. At other times I have witnessed sons and daughters watch their mother deteriorate because of cancer. I have seen children born handicapped, with cerebral palsy or muscular dystrophy.

How could I not be thankful to be healthy after seeing all of this? How could I not feel fortunate, even if my husband is incarcerated, after observing people dying and others that will never be helped? These experiences have opened my eyes. I've realized that my problem is not as great as others that are out there. I should feel lucky to be in the situation I'm in. So, while I'm still suffering a great deal of pain, others are suffering more. I could not continue going around complaining and making a big deal of my situation after witnessing suffering that at times was ten times greater than mine.

I visit periodically with the older clients who we serve. These visits are very special to me because, although the people I go to see are very sick, they make me feel wonderful. Sometimes I have my hair down when I go to visit them, and the first thing they say is, "Oh, you have such pretty long hair." And they touch my hair and then say, "You're so sweet, like a little girl." They're so loving; they touch me and hug me and hold my hand. They are so thankful that I do so much for them, but, in actuality, there is just so little to do to make them better. But their compliments are positive; they make a great deal of difference to me. I've seen how much courage thay have. They are so hopeful.

Going to visit some of the children I have in my program and seeing their smiles, smiles that I know were not there before—to see that the family has some kind of relief because they're receiving help from me and the program, to see that the family understands that I will try to do whatever is necessary because they know that I sympathize with them—all of these things make me feel rewarded. I enjoy working with the children and their families. There is a payoff for them as well as for me. I look at what I'm doing with these families as a system of reward because I'm receiving a great deal of satisfaction. I've come to realize that, in helping these children and the elderly, I'm helping myself. I have come to appreciate myself and my situation more. Some of their courage has rubbed off on me. I have become stronger because of them, and that makes for accepting and handling my situation with more ease.

5

Organizing against Injustice

After eight years of trying to control information to protect herself from being labeled as the wife of a prison inmate, Lourdes decided to put an end to her denial. She could no longer continue holding back in nearly every interaction she had with others.

During the long period of keeping silent many incidents of injustice and exploitation occurred, affecting family members of inmates as well as the inmates themselves, including her husband. Her regular weekly visits to the prison permitted Lourdes to witness the ongoing mistreatment by prison officials of Latinos who were there to visit a family member. Lourdes also observed the increasing number of young people from her neighborhood who were serving time. Conversations with inmates and family members, both inside and outside the wall, made Lourdes aware of the high number of broken marriages resulting from the imprisonment of husbands. On her visits Lourdes also saw the pressing need to improve prison conditions.

Against this backdrop Lourdes decided to go public—to join with other wives and mothers of inmates to find collective solutions. Lourdes finally accepted that her problems were really no different from those of other wives and mothers and that these shared problems could best be addressed, and perhaps resolved, by working together in a united front. Since 1990 Lourdes has worked extremely hard, sometimes against impossible odds, to organize and mobilize family members to find constructive and empowering ways of responding to their shared circumstances.

By at last going public, revealing her identity as a prisoner's wife, Lourdes took a first step on the way to initiating positive action for those like herself, who have a family member in prison.

I visit my husband on Saturdays. I look forward to Fridays because that's when my preparations for the visits actually begin. Fridays are hectic workdays. There are meetings to attend and reports to complete. At times I even visit some of our clients. So, waiting for Fridays to arrive sometimes does not make sense. How can someone be so eager for a hectic workday on Fridays? It's just that for me Fridays represent the day before the big day. I'm always looking forward to seeing my husband, and that's what Fridays symbolize. I can see beyond the workday.

Any other person would probably say: "It's the weekend. It's time to rest, to get chores done." That's not what I think about. I don't think about getting anything done on a Saturday. Saturday is the time when I actually get to see my husband. My thoughts on Fridays are that the following day I'm heading for the car ride and to be with him.

People would think that after nine years, almost ten, it wouldn't be like this. People would probably think that by now my mind would be on other things. But I definitely have not gotten to that point, and I don't think I ever will. In my mind I know that's what I have to do on Saturdays, and, if someone wants to do something on this day, I quickly say no.

Normally, other wives and girlfriends enjoy the privilege of seeing their loved ones every day when they come home from work. I don't have that privilege; I have to wait for one day in the week. So, from Sunday to Friday I feel all of this emotion building up—it's ready to burst out; I'm ready for Saturday. During the week I'm relaxed. I'm just coming home, going to school, going to church: there's nothing that I have to run home to. I don't really have to cook; there's no one waiting. So, all of this works up to Saturday. And on Saturday I make the best of it. So, I always look my best. I make sure that I never wear something that I wore during that same week. My Saturday visits with my husband are like weekly celebrations. It's a very special feeling.

Yet, Saturdays are very stressful. I need to make the hour or hour and a half I spend with my husband the best possible. It is like working up a high level of energy during the week for the Saturday visit. I make sure to talk to him about happy things and not anything troubling. I definitely go out of my way to be cheerful. I do this not only for my husband but for other inmates who are there too. I make sure I am always smiling and that I say hello because that's what they need to hear.

In my opinion I can't walk in there with a frown. This is not a place to go and say, "Okay, today we are going to argue and fight and settle the argument we had over the phone," though that may be needed at times. But the prison is not the place to do that.

I recognize how stressful this experience can be, yet I feel good about doing it. It makes me feel good because I took time to be a caring and loving wife. During the week I feel that sometimes I don't necessarily play the role of a wife because I don't come to be with my husband, to do things with him. He is not there; therefore, I do things for myself. In addition, my husband makes the experience very enjoyable. I know that he takes time to look the best for me. He is always clean-cut, always shaved, neat haircut, always smelling terrific, his pants are always ironed with a crease. He just looks very nice. So, immediately, I know he took time out to not just come out with his jeans and T-shirt like he just happened to get out of bed. I know he took time out to take a shower and look his very best.

Because of my hectic weekly routine, my mother somtimes has felt that I didn't have time to visit her or, for that matter, anyone else. I guess she was looking for me to socialize more with her and the rest of the family. She complained that I was just working, going to church, and visiting my husband on Saturdays and that that was my whole life. She thought I didn't have a life. I told her that I enjoyed what I was doing. I was able to go out once in a while, but, since I have never been or will never be a party person, I didn't miss it. This is exactly how she raised me; she didn't want me in parties, so parties were not important things for me. They still aren't. I don't feel like I'm missing anything because that's not the type of person I am. I may enjoy going out to dinner with friends, but, other than that, I'm not the kind of person who says: "Okay, it's Friday night. Let's go to a club and dance."

My Saturday morning begins like every other. I'm up at 6:30. If the weather is good, like during the summer, it takes me forty-five minutes to an hour to drive to the prison. In the winter the drive is longer. At other times it takes a little longer since I often pick up other people who do not have transportation. For a couple of years I was going by myself or with nieces or nephews. Now it's become a tradition to take someone with me, either a friend or the mother of someone who has to go over there. Sometimes my husband asks me to pick up a visitor because an inmate had not seen his family for a long time and he's in need of seeing someone. So, I go and pick up the wife, the mother, or whoever that person is. But to me all of it is worth it.

I don't mind driving other people. I only wish that I had a bigger car or a van because I know there are so many people who want to get out there. Although there's public transportation for people to go to the prison, the problem is that sometimes they don't know how or where to catch the bus. Taking the bus to the penetentiary is hard for some people because it runs on very strict schedules, and there are times when people miss it coming back because they're still waiting to be called to see their loved ones. So, if a person misses catching the bus at a particular time, it will be hours before the next bus comes. When a person goes on the bus that person must make the trip an all-day affair. That person could leave the house at six in the morning and not return home until six in the evening. So, many simply don't go; they just refuse to make the visits. Others wait until they find someone to carpool with, something that could take a long time, because, if they don't visit, how are they going to make contact with other families? It's a very tough situation. For sure, the visitor who is poor, the one who doesn't have transportation, never wins.

Driving with other women doesn't bother me because it's company; you have someone to talk to, and that makes the ride quicker. We share a lot. We have the same feelings; we are all going to the same place to deal essentially with the same situation. We are all feeling basically the same feelings of loneliness and separation. When we ride together we can talk about these feelings.

Driving with other women gives me the opportunity to learn about the way they think about what's going on at the prison. I get to discover if they are informed about the goings-on that take place inside. I learn about their husbands, sons, or boyfriends—what is happening with them and how they are being treated. And, of course, all of this leads to friendships with women who otherwise I never would have met.

Once we get to the prison, to the Wall, we have to walk up to a reception desk, which is like an information desk that is stationed right there at the front gate. It's at the front gate where I began to see the injustices that are associated with imprisonment. Visitors are treated nastily from that moment on. So, it's interesting because I become so excited about getting ready for the visit, for Saturday to come so I can see my husband, but, as soon as I get to the entrance of the prison, I must confront very quickly some cruel and insensitive group of individuals. It's like a bursting bubble. All of the excitement begins to disappear, but I try to be strong because I don't want to take a bad mood with me to see my husband. I want him to see me in good spirits.

What happens is that visitors have to register to go in. This process begins by us filling out a visitor's form. There is an officer who examines people's identification cards. After this the visitor goes to another desk, where another officer looks through the visitors' list to verify her name. Only those individuals whose names have been included in the visitors' list are allowed to visit an inmate. The problem begins when the visitor does not speak or understand English. All the instructions are in English, and some of our people just don't understand. For the guards the fact that some of our people do not speak English and can't fill out the forms is like, "Well, that's your tough luck." They don't care.

To me this is a way the institution uses to discourage us from visiting. The institution should hire bilingual officers; it's rarely that I've seen one of our people working there. Again, that is a way of saying: "Well, there is no one here who can help you. I'm sorry. See you later. It's not our problem that your man is here—that's your problem."

This is a terrible attitude to have toward us. It's obvious that the correctional system thinks that it is above the law, and no one can tell them how to run things, how to treat people. I cannot accept that. I cannot accept how we can't question them when, as taxpayers, the money to run these institutions is coming out of our pockets. We should have the right to say, "Well, this is happening, or that is happening." When we try to offer some suggestions or ideas so that people can come to visit or to improve conditions for the inmates, it's like: "We don't have the time to listen to you. Get out of here." So, visitors can't count on the system. We certainly can't rely on the officers for help. Maybe one out of a hundred is polite or sensitive. Very few will go out of their way to even say good morning to you. This is devastating for those of us who have been going there for so long. Why don't they say at least, "How are you doing?" The officers have this attitude that the men who are serving time are animals and that they don't have to respect these animals or their families.

The officers have this attitude, this belief, that the visitors are making them work more than what they should. They believe that they are doing the visitors a great favor by allowing us inside to see our loved ones. They really believe that we should be grateful, since, after all, we are there to see the scum of the earth. They talk loud at us. They want to make sure that we acknowledge that they are superior to us, that they are so much better than we are. Like I said earlier, there are very few that would say: "Good morning. How are you doing? Have a nice visit."

One day I was in line waiting to sign in to go see my husband when this Latina woman was having problems understanding what she was supposed to do. I stepped out of my place in line to help her, when the officer told me to get back in line. He said that this was none of my business, that he had not called on me for any help. I was shocked. I came to understand that I couldn't be of service at that moment. I did not ask to be paid for doing this deed, yet I was told that I wasn't needed.

There were other times when people were permitted to help because the officers found themselves in a desperate situation. They did not know how to communicate, and this was happening too frequently, and they were becoming annoyed. So, to save time and overcome their stress they would allow some of us to serve as interpreters.

For many of our people who can't speak English the only way for getting around this problem is to rely on other visitors. One result of this group reliance approach is that we have become a family.

So, almost involuntarily, not necessarily by our own choice, we have become united into a family of individuals who share the same things and who must help one another.

I have seen cases involving visitors who did not have the proper pieces of identification to get in because of new rule changes that they were not informed about. Sometimes these visitors drive all the way to the prison only to discover that, before they can be issued a visitor's pass, they needed three pieces of identification instead of two. In these cases they are told to go home. I have felt so bad. Why don't they allow these women in? The system doesn't write to us to inform us of the different changes in regulations they make. We only find out when we visit. This is really irritating. At that moment there was nothing that I could have done. That person, that woman, that mother or wife, had to turn around, drive another one or two hours and more without seeing the person she came to see.

In any event, once that initial procedure is taken care of your hand is stamped, and you go through to the shakedown room. In the shakedown room they check you to make sure you're not carrying a gun or drugs. There is a rule that states that visitors can't take into the prison more than thirty dollars. So, they check for that. They won't let you in if you have more than that amount. Some visitors who bring a large amount of money during the visit take it to their cars. But for those who take the bus they are not allowed to enter the prison and make the visit, since there's no place to keep the extra money. The officers would not agree to keep the extra amount of money so people can go on with the business they came there to do. The officers at the prison are really cold.

I know many people who oppose being shaken down. To them this is a very humiliating experience. Here are these guards searching people and touching their bodily parts. Not that the guards do this on purpose or all the time, but one consequence of being searched is that you could be touched where you don't want to be. People also feel a loss of self-respect because for them the search represents a symbol that they too are criminals, that they can't be trusted. This is hard for our people, who grow up in a culture of trust and faith. So, many prefer not to go to the prison on visits rather than to allow a search.

One good example is my stepfather. For all the many years my husband has been in there, my stepfather visited only once. It's not that he doesn't care about my husband; it's because he's paranoid. He simply doesn't like getting shaken down, and he doesn't approve of the system and how it works. All of this time I have tried telling him not to worry, because there is little about going through the shakedown. I tried doing everything that I possibly could to ease his concerns. I told him that they will ask him to take off his shoes and pat him down, that they were not going to strip-search him, yet he refused.

My stepfather has never been in trouble with the police. He has never gone to court or dealt with anything pertaining to trouble with the law. But the thought that to visit my husband he must deal with the police and guards makes him uncomfortable. So, he would ask me all the time to tell my husband to call him anytime and as much as he wants but that he is not going to the prison. My mother became angry one time and told him: "You have to get over this. Nothing is going to happen. You should go and see him because there are so many things happening. And God forbid that something happens to him or to you; then you will feel bad that you never took the time to go see him." It was then that he decided to go. This year was the first time he went out there, and my husband was really excited to see him.

I wasn't angry at my stepfather for refusing to visit my husband. I understand why he feels the way he does about the shakedown; at first I didn't like (to this day I still don't like) being searched, but it is something that I have had to deal with. For me it's quite simple:

in order to see my husband I must go through these people and their system. I had no choice in the matter; in order to see my husband I had to submit myself. That was my decision, but I couldn't force my stepfather to do the same. I'm glad my mother did.

I've also met ladies who will not allow themselves to be searched, even if this means not being able to see their husband or son. There's the grandmother of one of the inmates, whom she considers her son—she feels intimidated by being searched. As with my stepfather, I try to ease her mind by telling her it's routine and that everyone know she's not carrying anything. I tell her in Spanish, but she's always expressed discomfort about waiting so long and going through the shakedowns.

After the shakedown visitors go to another building, which is the administration building. To get there you have to walk through a courtyard. Each time I make this walk I always think, "When will be the last time?" I've come to know so many family members and guys through the years—I know that I will continue visiting and crossing this yard. Yet I'm anxious to walk through for the last time in terms of coming to visit my husband.

Once inside the administration building the officers who work this station give you a pass, and you write your name on a list, and you're directed toward the waiting room. You could be waiting there for as long it takes to bring the inmate into the visiting room. This could be a wait of one hour, two hours. Because you spend so much time waiting, you get to know people.

There is a television set in the waiting room, which is usually turned on all the time, so people watch television while they wait to be called. Others decide to read. And for others they spend the time talking. What is interesting is that, while we are all there for the same reason, people ordinarily don't want to talk to you. They don't want anybody to know, so it's pretty interesting to see people's expression.

Just from sitting in the waiting room week after week I would see the anguish in people's faces. It was like they were communicating how they couldn't handle dealing with the hostility of the guards and the overall administration of the prison. Since I have been going there for so long, people talk to me. So, for me the visits are like a family reunion. I walk in there and see people who I've come to know. We exchange hellos and begin to talk about how our weeks have been. I have always encouraged some of the women I've come to know well enough to call me and to tell me how I could help, because I could detect the pain they were suffering. Understandingly, some women simply would not say anything in the waiting room. So, our contact here would lead to telephone communication later on.

Whether in the waiting room or by phone, one thing that people would always ask me is how I've done it—how I've managed to survive all the years. They want to know how I've been able to sustain my marriage. To me that is such an important question, such an important issue that faces all of us. Many of our people feel that, under the circumstances of incarceration, it's very difficult to maintain a marriage. It is difficult because the wife now makes all the decisions. She can't turn to her husband, because there are times, when the husband is on lock-down, that he is not allowed to make phone calls or visit with people. The wife must become responsible for doing whatever the situation calls for. And, like the way I was before, many of our women have depended on their husbands for a long time.

Many women cry and tell me that they cannot do it because of their children. They believe they need a father figure for the children. Others believe they need help with the household; they are afraid of ending up on public aid. There are those who believe that a man is the only solution to their problems. So, it's very difficult when we are raised to think that way. Latina women are raised to be dependent all the time, so during times when we have to make for ourselves many of us can't do it.

What saddens me is that so many women give up on their marriages. I know about their hardships, but I don't think that they know how to deal with it. And that's why they just have to break off the marriage: they don't know how to deal with life while the husband is in there. Wives can't take living on the outside, with children and no husband.

I know of several cases involving broken marriages that resulted because of imprisonment, but there is one that is very close to my heart. It involves my own brother. It affected me enormously as well as my mother. I saw my mother destroyed.

Three months after my brother's sentence his wife, who was living with us, told us that she was moving in with her mother and was taking her daughter of six months. My mother feared the worst. My mother would tell her: "Well no, why don't you stay here? I want to be near my grandchild." But she made that decision. Unfortunately, when she went to live with her mother she ran into an old boyfriend of hers, and six months into my brother's sentence she became pregnant, still legally married to my brother. She tried to hide the pregnancy from us. Every time we went to pick up the little girl to bring her for my brother to see, she wouldn't want us to see her because of her huge stomach. It ended up that she left my brother, and my brother was let out within eighteen months, to a broken home. They were divorced.

But I must give him credit. He tried to make the marriage work after he was released. He is not a violent person; he was not incarcerated for a violent act. He went back to his wife and tried to work things out. What killed him was that when he would get up to go to work his little girl would say, "Why don't you kiss the baby, Dad?" He couldn't bring himself to say that he couldn't get close to another man's child, and, so, he couldn't take it; there was no trust. After three months he filed for divorce, and he's on his own now.

He's remarried, but what happened to him was ugly. She knew she was wrong. He has his daughter on weekends; he feels the child should be with the mother. I wondered how this could have happened. And to me I concluded that it was just so hard for her to be alone.

My husband had a family member like that who was incarcerated for seven years. He was serving an "underdog" mandatory sentence of one to fourteen years, which means that he could do half at a time. His wife waited about two years and then walked away. She took the kids and just left. Five years later, when he got out, she was remarried and had a child from someone else. She realized, she said, that she should have waited; she wanted to reconstruct the marriage, but it was too late. He only felt angry toward her because she left when he needed her the most. Those are the situations that I see, and they occur often.

From the waiting room we are finally called into the visiting room. There we spend about two hours talking with our loved ones.

Seeing and being with my husband is a good feeling. It's like I haven't seen him for so long. I see him every week, but not every day, so I always find him so much more handsome. I'm always looking at him; I always look for bruises. It's almost like a mother, checking to see that everything is in place.

For the time we spend together we simply talk. We are surrounded by many family members and friends who are there for the same reason. We talk about different things. If, for instance, we were talking on the phone during the week and the line was cut, we'll finish the conversation during the visit. We'll talk about the family. He's concerned about my health, finances, and work. He's also very concerned about what's happening on the outside. And I make sure he doesn't lose contact with what's happening. For every family gathering I take pictures and send them to him so he experiences life on the outside through them. For every event that we have as family he has pictures. I think that he has tons of photo albums.

One thing I talk about is that once he gets out I don't want life to be like it was. I continue to remind him that there's no way I would live that life again. It wasn't bad, but we were always surrounded by his friends. He says I was always first, but I didn't see it that way. So, now I feel that I'm owed a lot. And, when he comes out I don't want to run his life, but I want to let him know and understand that it's our time. We have a lot to make up for. There's a lot of walks in the park we missed out on because he was afraid to walk in the streets because of gang violence. There are a lot of things we couldn't do as a husband and wife—go to the beach, go on a carriage ride downtown. There's a lot of things to make up for.

When I tell my husband about things that we didn't do he says that I'm right. The memories bring a lot of hurt to him, but he knows that I'm telling him the truth. That's exactly how I feel. He tells me that things are going to be different, and inside our minds the goal is to make things different for us and for the people around us. Our goal is to prevent others from having to go through the pain we have experienced for so long. I have said that, if I had a chance to live my life again, that I may change some things but not much. I wouldn't change many things because I've learned so much. I would not have gained this knowledge that I have if it had not been for all the downfalls. It has been a tough way of learning life, but the experience and knowledge I have gained are priceless. Those are things I can give to someone else. I'm of the opinion that something very positive is going to come out of this; it's not going to be all pain and suffering.

In a recent PBS [Public Broadcasting Service] documentary, Throwaway People, *in which an African-American community in Washington, D.C., is examined for its historic deterioration, a community worker who refuses to give up on the area and its residents is heard saying: "Most of our talented*

*young men are learning about life in prison. Young men, who in years past
represented pillars for the next generation, are now inmates. Fewer and
fewer young men are found living normal lives in our community."*

*These impressions are echoed in communities throughout the United
States in which African American and Latino/as make up the majority of the
population. The case of the Division Street area fits this portrayal: many of
its young men, who could be attending school and learning how to participate in conventional life, are in prison. Lourdes's husband is one such person—and so are the hundreds of inmates Lourdes sees on her weekly visits to
the penitentiary.*

In the visiting room while visiting with my husband I can't help but
to notice the large number of young people who are serving time.
Sometimes I wish I would not have to see anyone else. I want to
spend an enjoyable time with my husband, but these young people
are everywhere. They appear to be all around me. There are over
thirty young men from my community serving time in the prison
where my husband is being held. These are the same people who I
grew up with, people who I've known for a long time. I would
suspect that many more can be found throughout the system. Just
imagine that: over thirty young minds that were not nurtured to be
of service to our community—how can this be? A good part of our
community has been transplanted to a prison system. So, while with
my husband, I have to acknowledge those other individuals around
us.

I'm talking about people who were seventeen years old when
they started serving time, guys that didn't even know what life was;
they had not experienced life yet. They were children when they
first got locked up. That individual has not been a husband or a
father and may never be.

Right now the solution to the so-called gang problem is to build
more prisons so more members can be locked up. It's getting to the
point where the state is simply warehousing these guys, converting

them into a production line. Young men from our community, who look and think more like children, are being made into a cheap labor force for the state. If the state can get an inmate to do some renovation work, for example, and it doesn't have to pay him ten to twelve dollars, like it would have to for someone else, that is a big plus. If the state wants to pay that inmate just a pack of cigarettes, who is to say that it's wrong? Nobody is there monitoring this.

Our youngsters are the victims. I know quite well that the guys in our neighborhood are not little angels, but I'm opposed to the idea that an eighteen-year-old should be sentenced to prison for life. We should be about preventing these acts from happening in the first place and not about looking to see who did what so they can be locked up for the rest of their lives. That's ridiculous.

I think that youngsters are victims because they are too young to know about the consequences of living a life of dealing drugs or being involved in a gang. They do not understand what the major consequence is—that they are going to have to pay with their lives. It's part of the problem that we have right now. What I'm saying is that many of these young men who are in prison are there because they committed a crime without knowing what that was going to get them. This may sound like a ridiculous interpretation for some people, but it's reality. It takes imprisonment for these guys to realize what they have done. By then it's too late because the door has closed behind them, and they are not getting out.

When I spoke to the other women who had a family member in prison another topic they would always mention were the conditions that the inmates were facing. On many occasions mothers would call me and say that the institution told them that her son was the property of the state and that they could do anything they want with him, so the son would be transferred to another prison without the family knowing. The institution tells the mother that they can't give out that information and to call at another time.

One of the first of these cases occurred several years ago. It involved the woman who drives with me every week. She told me that the family felt very insulted because the institution could have contacted them since people there speak English very well and are well educated. Instead, this woman had to call Springfield to find out where her son was. They found out that he was moved because of a fight between inmates and officers. He was placed on a circuit. When an inmate is placed on a circuit this means that he is constantly transferred from institution to institution because he is considered high risk or uncontrollable.

What the system wants to do is ensure that the inmate cannot adjust at any institution. So after thirty days in one institution the inmate must pack up and leave for another. In the case of this woman's son, he was badly injured while on circuit. He suffered a broken arm during a fight with another inmate; he was in terrible pain. He couldn't write because of his broken arm. Because an inmate is not permitted to have telephone privileges while on a circuit, he couldn't call and make contact with his family.

So, the family got frustrated. They called Springfield. Officials there told them that he was uncontrollable and that he was the property of the state and that they could transfer him any time they wanted without contacting them or justifying what they were doing.

I sat there listening to this woman tell me this story, and my mouth was wide open; it wanted to drop. "How cruel can they be?" It is cruel to the family and the individual. If the state wants to say that inmates are property, well, that's fine—but that person has a family out here, and they have a right to know what's happening to him. They can't say he belongs to them and not to the family, and that's literally what they say in these cases. That is cruel and heartless.

Women also talked to me about drug abuse inside the prison and their fear for their sons and husbands. They were afraid that prisoners were using drugs and something really bad could happen.

That's exactly what I experienced with an inmate with whom I was very close.

Two years ago I got that frightening call, the call that nobody wants to receive, because it's usually about something bad that happened to your husband, brother, or friend. On 4 January 1988, at about 4:30 A.M., I was called by the institution and was asked if I was Edwin's sister, and I said that I was. Edwin was a young man who was like a brother to me; he had no father or mother. He was serving time in another institution. My first thought was that they were transferring him, but, instead, they told me, "I'm sorry to inform you that he has passed away." That was so hard to deal with.

I didn't know what to do. A young man at the age of twenty-nine died due to an overdose of drugs in prison. He suffered a massive heart attack and died. And to think that he died by himself in a cell—that was the worst thing that could have happened.

I started gathering the family. I contacted his sister in Puerto Rico. It was hard for her because they were separated at an early age, and it was hard because of financial struggles for her to come here. He also never wanted for her to come and see what conditions he was living under, so every form of communication had been done through the mail.

Taking the body and giving him proper burial took a lot out of me, to the point where I just didn't want to go on. My husband would tell me the opposite: "You need to go on." Then the worst part of it all was that my husband was allowed to come out to pay his respects during the burial, because Edwin was raised with my husband's mother as an adopted son. So, here I was, trying to handle the whole situation and look at this one person whom I loved so much, and then to see my husband being brought in by two police officers. They had my husband handcuffed, shackled, hands and feet, and I was struggling with these two pains, wondering which one was worse.

I thank God because I was able to finish off by finding Edwin's brother, whom Edwin was never able to find himself. Edwin's brother has Down's syndrome and is in a Waukegan [Illinois] health center, and I have just become his guardian. I think that Edwin would be satisfied if he knew that there's someone taking care of and seeing after his brother. Unfortunately, Edwin never got the satisfaction of knowing that his brother was alive; he thought he was dead. Although Edwin's brother doesn't know much of anything, being there for him gives me a sense that you have to go on, and when one is gone you pick up the pieces with someone else.

I still think of how Edwin was able to get his hands on drugs; that's still a mystery. The system concluded that someone had brought them to him; that he got them from an inmate or a visitor. But to me there is more than this simple explanation, although I can't prove anything. But it's publicly known that correctional officers have been charged with drug trafficking. These officers are making money, tons of it, by selling drugs. Why do you think they stay in their jobs? I'm sure it is not to wait for every week to receive a paycheck. So, it's not surprising how the drugs get in. It's not something the system likes to hear or likes to acknowledge. I feel they need to recognize the problem they have in their hands so then maybe they can prevent other people from taking their lives.

After seeing all of these things happening, after seeing the amount of injustice suffered by other women and family members because of who they are, I just said, "Something has to be done for the Latinas out there." After nine years of frustration I decided to take action. As Latinas, we have a culture that has such a deep feeling for our loved ones, and when someone is imprisoned or when someone dies we just don't know how to deal with it sometimes. So, that's when I said we have to do something, get together, and God only knows when my husband is going to get out, so I have to do something now.

I thought of an organization, a referral service where wives, mothers, and other family members could come with their questions and concerns. I thought that we could start with a support group. We all knew that we needed to be realistic and get involved because the situation for our husbands, sons, and the young people in our community was not going to get any better.

I started talking to other wives, and I discovered that where they needed assistance was really for basic things. For example, they would call me to ask how to get to the institution; they didn't know the way to the prison. Others would just ask me to give them a ride because they didn't have any transportation. I would tell my husband these things, and he would in turn tell other inmates, and then they would tell their wives and friends, and before long everyone was calling me for the same things. The calls kept coming, and I had to turn people down; no one else could fit in my car because I didn't have a CTA [Chicago Transit Authority] bus. I wish I did; then everyone could come along.

In my mind I started taking this different course to the whole situation two years ago. I was hesitant because, if I got too vocal, too involved, something terrible was going to happen. But what more can happen? I've gone through it all. I've dealt with the death of someone whom I loved very much. My husband is still in there, and so are other loved ones. I've gone in there, and I've seen my friends being brought out because their mothers died, and they've been brought out to to the funeral. So, I've seen so much—what else can happen?

My husband and other inmates played an important role in encouraging me to develop the organization. They also gave me the information that I needed to justify developing the organization. Because I don't live in the prison, I only see things from the outside; I really don't see what is happening on the inside. So, I was able to gather a lot of information from them. It was more than having them tell me what was happening with their lives; most of us already knew that. They did a great deal of research and showed me actual evidence of what they were talking about. They gave statistical reports on the increases in the inmate population. The reports showed the racial breakdown of the inmates—like, for instance, most are black or Latino. The reports talked about the overcrowding that the system does not want to acknowledge. There were reports showing how the taxpayers' money was being invested into building more prisons, rather than on programs to help with the situation of the inmates. They showed how the state is budgeted, what the cost is for each inmate, the amount of money inmates get paid, and the types of labor they perform. I think that, eventually, I would have gotten that information myself, but they got it to me quicker. I give them a lot of credit for the work they did.

Inmates are never taken seriously or given credit for what they know. Many of these guys are pretty together and smart; after all, what they all have on their hands is time, and a lot of them use it wisely. They dedicate themselves and hit the books really hard. Not everyone is in prison to pump iron. There is also the case that some of them are looking for a way out, so that means that they are going to be in the law library twenty-four hours a day reading and doing research. But, again, to do that they must be able to read and understand well what they are reading.

Once we started building the organization I began to see how it mirrored a family. Although the women in the organization [male participation was very limited] didn't have the same blood running through our veins to tie us together as a family, we were building a very special family relationship. Like a family, there developed a structure of bonding that was built around a commitment of trust toward one another. We became close as a family because we also came from a structure of family bonding.

There is more. The idea of the family means that we all share the same common condition: as Latinas and women, we have a relative, a loved one, who is incarcerated, and, because of that inmate, most of us are going through difficult hardships. As a family, then, we rely on one another. We have someone that confides in us and with whom we can talk. So, we believe that, as a family, the organization will work to represent and protect our feelings. We are going to put all of our strengths together to support ourselves. As a family, we are going to laugh together, and we are going to cry together.

As a family, we also want to make the statement to prison officials that we are human beings and deserve respect, that we need to be treated with dignity, that just because our relative is incarcerated does not mean that we should be treated with any less respect. It all begins here.

I hope to accomplish a lot as a family. We can unite and be there for one another. For those inmates who may not have family support we can adopt them; we can be there for them. We can set up a pen pal writing system to provide inmates with a voice and ear from the outside. We also hope to let the system know at every institution that programs can be developed with the residents and the family so as to ease the hostility that exists between families and the system. It's believed that the prison where my husband is kept is the worst institution in the state, and that's because they treat the inmates like animals, as if they don't have or deserve any rights. That particular institution doesn't give inmates any kind of breathing room. They just lock them up in their cells, and that's it.

Through the organization I'm certain that I'm not going to be able to change everything. I'm just trying to make prison officials realize that, through some programs, things can change in a positive way. For example, some prisons allow families to have picnics together, and the fathers have the opportunity to play with their children. The prison where my husband is doesn't have that. For inmates to be in a more relaxed atmosphere, even if it's only for an hour, can make a world of difference to them. I hope that they will hear us. I know that I have a lot of faith in a lot of things, but I believe that nothing is impossible. I'm sure that there are answers to the things we are requesting, and, if we present them in a positive way, they will listen to us.

We also want the system to recognize us more. We want to have some say in the decision-making process involving our relatives. We want to tell the administration that it doesn't have the sole rule about its so-called property to use and misuse as it pleases. We want them to acknowledge that they have people to answer to, whether they like it or not. There are mothers and wives who need to be answered to and be accountable to. I can't accept that someone is going to come and tell me, "You have to accept the condition, and there is nothing that you can say or do about it." I can't accept that.

Since we started having meetings, about seven families have participated. I was anticipating larger numbers, but I understand. Latina women feel intimidated because they think the worst: they think that we're going to go out there screaming and picketing and that something is going to happen. I try to assure them that that won't happen. Also, for so long they have been informed that, if they rock the boat, conditions are only going to get worse. Many women have accepted this and have said no to our call. They all tell me the same thing: "Something is going to happen to my son. Something is going to happen to my husband. He's going to be transferred, and right now he is not that far away." They prefer to leave things as they are.

With seven families we have started the process. It was essential to begin by recognizing publicly that we are the wives or mothers of prison inmates. Initial meetings were dedicated to this kind of discussion. And when a new person shows up for a meeting we take time to talk to her about the importance of recognizing and acknowledging her situation as the wife of an inmate.

I've learned that nothing can be done until the woman accepts the fact that her husband [or son or other family member] is serving time. I was not able to do very much, not able to communicate anything to anyone, until I accepted who my husband was and what had happened to him. I've accepted the fact that he is a gang leader, a gang member who is in prison. It's very hard when a woman has to admit to people that her husband is in prison. I tell the members that it's not like they have to give other people their entire life history. I ask them to limit the conversation but to keep their integrity as women and human beings. And that's all I ask them to do, because carrying this pain inside for so many years can ultimately lead to separation from their husbands.

In the meetings the overriding topic discussed is the treatment family members receive from the officers and administration when they visit the prison. All the members have expressed having been treated unfairly. They want to see some changes. They want to know what they can do to change this problem.

We also talk about the hate that women sometimes feel toward their husbands. Wives and mothers go through a great deal of pain—namely, the pain of being separated from a loved one. There is also the pain of adjustment. Then comes the loneliness—people are always asking, "How am I going to deal with life by myself?" And, of course, the women want to know when all of this is going to end. In the meantime they hate their husbands for having done this to them; they hate their husbands for putting them in this situation.

Surprisingly, after the conclusion of the meetings and after we have some coffee I see people smiling. They walk in the meetings looking tired or sometimes with a chip on their shoulder, saying, "Like, I'm so mad." But after those two hours I see them walking out with a smile because, although we might not have accomplished a great deal, at least we were able to let it all out. To let it all off our chests helps enormously. People feel more relaxed because they were able to talk about what was bothering them, and we all understood because we are all going through the same thing.

Above everything else I really believe that the essence of the organization is allowing people to get off their chests the heavy pain and anger they carry around with them. Even if the person goes home after the meeting and cries, at least for a while she let it out because there was someone else at the meeting who understood what she is going through. It's not the same thing telling someone your feelings when they have not gone through the same experience. So, the women are like, "Wow, this was good."

A good example of this involves a recent experience I had with my supervisor at work. I was talking to her about my husband, and I told her things she didn't know about. She didn't know that he was a gang leader. And she was like, "Aren't you mad at him?" I said: "Yes, I was. I'm not mad at him anymore." I saw the anger in her face. She was really angry because I was going through all of this for a gang member who is incarcerated. Well, that's precisely the feelings of people who don't have anyone in prison. They are like, "How could he do that?" or "How could she put up with that?" So, it's important for wives and mothers to be able to come and talk with someone who has been through that, someone who is not going to be critical or judgmental, who is going to be sympathetic. That's the major difference: in our organization we have people who are very sympathetic and supportive.

This experience has made my husband and me grow an enormous amount. I went from being eighteen years of age to forty in no time. I don't really feel old; rather, I feel matured. When I tell people my age their reaction is, "Really?" And I say, "Yeah, don't I look my age?" Their answer is that I look older. They don't mean older in the sense of being an old person; instead, they mean someone who is wise. After I hear this I tell them, "I see—okay." It's a good feeling knowing that people think of you in those terms. I too feel wise. Sometimes I can't believe that I have learned so much in such a short period of time.

Being mature helps me when I talk to the group. They know that they are listening to someone with experience and wisdom. They are receptive to what I tell them. I might be talking about the importance of not getting married until the persons are very certain. I tell them that love is a beautiful thing but to make sure of what they are doing.

I feel very grateful; life has taught me a lot. I think that, if it weren't for this experience, I would not be independent, able to make my own decisions. Because of this experience, I have become empowered. Like I said before, this may sound like a terrible way for a person to become empowered, but I guess we each do it differently. Some people deal with imprisonment differently than others. Though I live under so many hardships and fall asleep crying, I realize I have to go on; I cannot wait for someone to do things for me. To me this is being empowered.

I saw one of my husband's brothers, who could not deal with him being incarcerated. He went on to become a heavy drinker and drug abuser. I would sit with him and tell him that he could not do this to himself. He would tell me that he won't stop until his brother gets out. I'm like: "How dare you? You cannot do this. You will not see him get out. He will come out and see you ten feet under. Look at me—I'm the wife. I shared the last few moments of his life [before prison] with him." He gets me angry that he cannot deal with the situation. I tell him he has to be strong, and for me too, but he has not been able to deal with the situation. He has a beautiful family. He's on his second marriage, and he has three children from his first wife and four from his second wife; he just had a set of twins. I point this out to him—that he has a lovely family, that he has to stop doing this—but he doesn't think he has a problem. Unfortunately, he does.

What I'm trying to say is that people deal with imprisonment in different ways. For me it has given me power I did not have before. I feel stronger.

The Fight Continues

Lourdes's most persistent fear became a reality in the summer of 1991: her husband was transferred to a prison outside of the state of Illinois. A disturbance involving inmates and guards had erupted at the prison where her husband was being held, and prison officials assumed he had masterminded or instigated it. Prison officials reached the conclusion that Lourdes's husband's role in provoking the disturbance called for severe punishment, and he was moved to another state.

For Lourdes the action taken by prison officials represented another devastating blow to her already painful and difficult existence. It also signaled the particular outcome she knew could result from her involvement in issues related to prison inmates and their families. Lourdes was certain that her husband's transfer to a penetentiary in another state was a sign by prison officials that they disapproved of her organizing initiatives.

When officials decided to move Lourdes's husband she became more convinced than ever about the essential value of the work she was carrying out on behalf of inmates and their family members. More than any other time before Lourdes recognized the value of her efforts in helping to establish a more humane and dignified system for inmates and their families, one that guarantees them the fair treatment they deserve as human beings. Rather than succumbing to what she saw as unjust treatment by prison officials, Lourdes responded by working harder than ever to facilitate her husband's release. While plans for an appeal involving her husband's case had been underway for some time, Lourdes now understood the urgency of speeding up the process to prove her husband's innocence and return him to the outside world. Before this could happen, however, she needed to have her husband returned to the state of Illinois, where such a trial would be held. Because prison officials had firmly decided to keep her husband in a different state, this became a tremendous emotional and psychological battle for Lourdes.

Everything was basically falling into place during spring 1991. I was looking forward to establishing the organization on more solid ground. I came to realize that to build an organization requires a great deal of patience because that process is very slow and it involves many people and their concerns. People who show an interest in joining the efforts that we want to pursue through the organization have to get to know one another. People must be made to feel confident and at ease with each other, and this takes a long time. Some people thought that this was another organization and that very little was going to be accomplished, so I needed to convince these people that for sure we were going to do some very important things. Other people thought that they didn't have the time to meet; people thought that changing a system that had been in place for so long was virtually impossible—these were some of the things that we needed to hammer out.

Because of the concerns of the people, I realized that I had to present to them at meetings convincing arguments about why it was important to get involved. I think that I did. I would tell them that our purpose as an organization was not to get the key to the front door and make these massive changes. I couldn't think along those lines. All I wanted to do was to make people realize that we didn't deserve the treatment we were getting. I wanted them to know that the inmates were being treated unfairly and that, although they were inmates, the system needed to respect them.

Also, there were some divisions inside the prison, among the inmates, over the control of the organization. Some people there thought that they could monopolize or control the organization for their own interests. There were others who thought that I was being used by my husband. I never lost sight of the work that some of the inmates did in terms of providing some of the information we used to convince family members that we needed to organize ourselves. However, I felt insulted by their behavior. I had said from the very beginning that this was not my organization but, rather, it was an organization of the people and for the people. None of the inmates were going to control the organization from the inside. This was going to be an organization that outside people were working very hard to put together, and it was going to be that way and remain that way. For me it was quite simple: it was our organization; it did not belong to anyone else.

So we had started the organization the year before, and things were beginning to look up. I found families coming together more often. I was extremely enthusiastic about its future, about its potential for making the lives of inmates more tolerable. At least this is how I was thinking at that time.

My relationship with my husband was very good. He was communicating more than ever with me. He was making preparations to have his case appealed. I was helping him. My husband had become very skillful in looking up and studying cases of imprisonment. He learned a lot about the law while he was serving time in Illinois. He had gotten to know very well the language of the law from working at the prison library for several years. He would tell me of the books he used to read that pertained to law cases. He also had taken courses at a junior college through a program that the penetentiary has. So, everything he learned over the years was going to be put into practice through the preparation for his appeal.

While we were involved making preparations for his case, we were working hard in trying to identify an attorney who we could trust. We wanted to find someone who was willing to listen to what my husband and I had to say because, when my husband was first convicted, we had very little say in terms of how the case was put together. And, of course, many things were not presented during the case. This time around my husband felt that he had things to tell that he couldn't have said before. So, he was very hopeful that things were going to work out.

I was very happy about his hopefulness. I felt good knowing that he was so optimistic, yet I didn't want to think about it too much. We had already gone through one appeal that didn't go the way we had wanted. I didn't want to build up my hopes again. I just wanted to take it a day at a time. I guess I was trying to be protective of my feelings. I didn't want to be overwhelmed about another negative experience. I couldn't take another defeat.

Of course, I don't share these feelings with my husband. He feels too excited and enthusiastic for me to lower his morale and enthusiasm. And maybe in the situation that he is in he needs to think positively and enthusiastically about some things. His optimism helps him to cope and to deal with each day. Knowing that his appeal case will go well gives him reasons for feeling good. I don't want to take those feelings away from him. They are very important for his own survival.

During May our church held a convention, and I had just finished serving a two-year term as vice president of the Midwest District for Ladies of the Assemblies for Christian Churches. At the convention I was elected to be president. I had anticipated the nomination, and I wasn't certain whether I wanted to accept it. There were so many things that I was involved in. In addition, I really didn't think I was going to be nominated because there were other people who I thought could do a better job. But I was nominated by such a large majority that I couldn't have refused. The voices of so many women were calling me forward to accept becoming their president. I couldn't say no to the way people reacted. I also enjoy the church so much, so accepting the nomination was evidence of my feelings toward the church. To me it's the church that gives us power and reason to keep going. In our lives sometimes we don't have avenues of support—to me the church represents that. So, I wanted to serve it because it is so important for so many people.

There is more. I accepted the nomination because I like challenges. This nomination gave me something else to set my mind on and something new to work on. During the course of the year the president works very hard, visiting different churches and making sure that programs are carried out properly. But, overall, the president must do the work in a way that everyone is pleased. This is a major challenge because the president has to work with over two hundred or three hundred ladies, and they all have different personalities and characters. In addition, there are groups made up of young people and other groups made up of older people. How do you keep all of these individuals and groups happy and satisfied? This is essentially what the president is supposed to do. I felt like I was taking on a major challenge and responsibility, and I wanted to do a good job at it.

In July the ladies' organization had the first jubilee, in which I served as their president. All the ladies in the organization from the different churches that make up the large umbrella organization of Christian Churches were present. We have four jubilees a year; each is held on the first Saturday of every third month. A jubilee is a very spiritually filled, religious service. It's a major conference, which begins with the presentation of reports indicating what's happening in each church, what people expect to happen during the course of the next three months, and what the president is expected to do. This is followed by an evening service, where usually a preacher, who always is a pastor, leads the service. After this there is a program where the ladies take part.

Once elected president I told my board that, while we have fantastic male pastors, we also have talented ladies that we need to use in the capacity of presenting lectures and sermons. For me what I wanted to do was very simple: I wanted to use the ladies who we had to do things that we had not been called to do before. I wanted them to give a conference and do the preaching. I told them, "We aren't going to use male pastors because we are talented enough to do the job ourselves." I felt that our talents as ladies needed to be recognized outside of the traditional roles we had played. I wanted one of our ladies to speak from the pulpit, to assume the powerful role of informing us of her ideas.

Needless to say, the women speakers were terrific. It was just a glorious day. What made for the glorious day was the fact that everyone was bubbly without using the bubbles. Everyone was feeling really good. This good feeling comes from within, and this feeling comes from our beliefs. It comes from the Holy Spirit that dwells among us. The feeling that we experience during the jubilees represent the inner peace that we feel at that particular moment. We feel good because we realize that we are together with ladies that we will not see for another three months because they belong to other churches or congregations. To hear the word of God gives us that special feeling. It makes us realize that we can be one woman or man talking out there, but the message can be interpreted differently by different individuals. So, what happens is that everyone leaves the jubilee thinking "that message was just for me."

At this jubille the wife of one of the pastors of one church was the speaker. She is a very timid, very shy woman. She barely says hi and good-bye to people. But she is truly a sweet lady. When I presented her name to the board for consideration as a possible speaker, they were all like, "She doesn't speak." I told the members of the board that she was the one I wanted to use. When I called her to ask her to give the conference or speech at the jubilee, she accepted. She gave this beautiful conference. It was a talk about being a Christian wife. She said that, just because we are Christian wives, it doesn't mean that we are not women—that we need to express our feelings, that we need to tell our husbands what bothers us and what doesn't. She even talked about our sexual needs and the fact that we can't be afraid to discuss them, even if the woman is the wife of a pastor. She was using herself as an example of the things she was talking about.

In the Christian tradition talking in the open about sex is taboo. Sex is only for the bedroom, and we are not supposed to talk about it. Some of the pastors really think like that. In the conference she gave this woman was open about the topic. She wasn't too explicit, but she generalized about many things. It was quite nice. The ladies left feeling really good. It gave them something to think about.

Of course, I too was feeling very upbeat. I saw the jubilee as a major success. I felt that we had accomplished what we set out to do. At the end of conference I left for home. I was physically tired and needed to just rest. I was anxious to get to my house, take off my shoes and throw myself in the bed.

I couldn't have imagined what was waiting for me at home. When I got home that evening, around eleven o'clock, I learned that a "riot" had broken out at my husband's penetentiary and an inmate had been killed. I also learned that an officer had been hurt as well. I had no idea of specific details because, when something like this happens, the whole prison system goes on a lock-down. Phone calls are not allowed during this period. Since I couldn't make contact with my husband, I didn't know how he was. I was very frustrated.

The next day [Sunday] I called my pastor and told him that I was not going to church because I needed to go to the state penetentiary to find out what was happening. Once there I was not able to see my husband because they had taken him out on a court hearing or something like that. They wouldn't give me any information, so I had to leave. I don't know what my feelings were at the time. I didn't know what to think. I had no idea or reaction. I needed to talk to my husband to find out what was going on because the administration was not going to tell me anything. They told me to return the following day, which was Monday.

The next day I called work and told them I wasn't coming in because I needed to find out what was going on in the prison. I was able to see my husband on Monday. I could tell by the look on his face that he was very upset. I became very concerned. I was happy that I saw him and he was okay. He told me the other guys were basically okay, but he didn't know what was going to happen next.

I felt a little better after seeing my husband. I was still uneasy because he was uneasy. He kept telling me: "These people are harassing us. They want us to tell them things we have no knowledge about, and they are harassing us, particularly the Latinos because it was a Latino that got killed." So, he gave me the impression that he was uneasy.

I told him to remain in control. I asked him to try to stay calm and not to let anything get to him. My other concern was that something was going to happen and I would not know anything about it. I thought of him possibly getting hurt. I thought of the guys getting hurt. I didn't want the guards to hurt them like they do when they think the inmates need to be punished. Usually, what the guards do is to make them experience a lot of mental torture by constantly harassing them. Other times the guards punish them physically in such a way that bruises are not detected. For example, the guards have this practice of putting handcuffs on the inmates very tight. This causes a great deal of pain; however, the inmate cannot complain since there is no evidence of physical brutality.

I got really down. I came to work, and my superiors, of course, were asking me about my faith, and I tried to explain to them that I have faith but I needed to do what I had to. I was worried, and I couldn't say: "Okay, I heard on the news that there was a riot and maybe no one is alive, and I couldn't just go to work and worry about it on the following Saturday. I couldn't do that."

The next Saturday I went back, and this time they had my husband in handcuffs because he was under investigation, along with a number of other inmates. The first thing I said was, "What is happening?" My husband was under investigation because apparently the disturbance happened in his cell house. There are different houses in the prison; the riot happened in his house. So they wanted to investigate everyone. The practice of putting handcuffs on inmates and having the inmates make visit calls while handcuffed is a form of discipline that the system uses to harass, embarrass, and overall bring more mental torture to the inmates. What the system is telling the inmates is, "Well, if you don't want your family to see you like this, then don't get out of line."

When I saw my husband being brought out with handcuffs I was shocked. I didn't know what to think. I didn't know if he had done anything. I just had to ask him. We sat down, and he told me not to worry. He just said that a number of inmates from the same cell had been placed in segregation, and they were all being investigated.

Being identified by the administration as a key person in what's happening at the prison is something that won't escape an inmate. When an inmate is marked he's marked no matter what he tells them. They will always consider that inmate a troublemaker. Of course, my husband was a marked inmate. My husband was questioned about the incident and essentially responded by communicating what he knew of it, which wasn't what the administration wanted to hear. The administration felt that my husband simply didn't want to cooperate. The administration wanted my husband to tell them, "Oh, yes, I send this individual to do that," or, "Yes, I am the one who controls this institution and gives the orders." But my husband couldn't tell them any of this because he had nothing to do with the incident. So, they transferred him.

The next week he was taken to a correctional center downstate by Springfield [Illinois]. I saw him there. I had taken vacation from work that week. I was going to St. Louis to see my sister—so, I was going that way anyway. My vacation turned out to be spending three days in this little town where I knew no one. I saw my husband for three days, and then I went to my sister's for the rest of the time.

That's how my vacation was spent, seeing him in a new place. I came back home relieved, knowing that he was doing okay. I thank God for that. My thought at the time was that he was going to be okay. I thought that, since he was in a new place, and even though it was a little distant, things were going to be alright. I didn't think it was going to be bad. I also thought that this move was temporary and that he would be returned shortly.

Two weeks later he calls me and tells me that they are still bothering him, asking that he tell them what had happened. He said that he kept telling them the same things he had told them earlier, and they were responding very nasty to him. He said that they were talking about transferring him out of state. I told him, "They can't do that, so don't worry." I felt that transferring him out of the state was not possible. I had seen people been transferred within the Illinois system, so I didn't think they would go to the extreme of taking him out of the state. All of this time I thought that the transfer would occur within the system, that he would be placed in a circuit and be rotated around within the system. "There are so many facilities—why would they want him to go somewhere else?" This is how I was thinking at the time.

I came home one day, and my brother, who was staying with me at the time, and my *compadre* [godfather], who is now in Puerto Rico, were sitting at the dining room table waiting for me. As soon as I came inside the house, they asked me to sit down. I asked them to tell me why they were asking me to sit down, and they just said that they had a question to ask me. So, I said, "Why, what's wrong?" They made it seem like nothing was happening. They always do this to me. So, they asked me if an inmate can be transferred out of state. I thought I knew everything and said, "Of course not," but then at the same time I was thinking, "Why are they saying this?" I asked them: "Is everything okay? Why are you asking me this?" My brother just said that he only had a question about the matter. But, in reality, he wasn't telling me the truth, because my husband had brought up the topic to his attention also. They were concerned with how I was going take it if he was transferred out of state.

I wasn't surprised over the fact that my husband was concerned about my welfare. That's the way he has always been. His concern is me. He thinks that if I'm okay, then he is okay. So, if something happens to me, it's going to happen to him as well. In his mind he has to be convinced that I'm alright.

At one time in our lives I didn't think that our relationship would ever get to this point. I'm a bit worried, however, over the way he thinks, because I simply cannot be okay at all times. I always try to tell him that. I try telling him not to be so dependent on me. If I get sick, I just get sick—that's nature. I remind him that, if I die, well, I just die. His reaction is, "No, don't say that." I try to kid around with him because I try to make him realize that life sometimes can be cruel. Sometimes things happen that people don't expect. So, if it happens that I die, I tell him that he could always find himself a new wife. But he always says the same thing: "No, don't say that, not even kidding around."

During the the third week in August his sister and one of his brothers wanted to go down to see him. That day I got up, and I had this feeling like something was wrong, so I called in work to tell them I wasn't coming in. I was worried about his sister and brother going there. I couldn't help but to feel like something was going to go wrong. That's why I always say that I do things because of my instincts. It's like my body is telling me that I'm sick. I decided to stay home because I was anticipating something to happen that day.

So, what happens? At nine his sister called. She sounded really upset. She told me that he wasn't there and they wouldn't tell them where he was at. I was like, "What do you mean he's not there?" I was frantic. Since I have a two-way line on my phone, I put her on hold and called the front desk of the institution at Springfield and asked where my husband was. The person at the desk said, "We can't give you that information right now. He's in transfer." I asked, "Where did you take him?" They gave me the number for the transfer coordinator unit in Springfield, and I called him. I was talking to this person, and he was like, "I understand, but I can't tell you right now because we risk security if we tell you where he is going right now. You are gonna have to wait." When I learned that the institution was not going to give any information, I told my husband's sister and brother to come home.

I was thinking, "My God, how can they do this?" I felt so lost. I was living again those horrible moments of the initial trial when he was sentenced. I was living again the first moments when we were separated. It was terrible. Within an hour my house was filled with people. The family had come over; my mother-in-law was there, my *comadres* [godmothers]—they were all there. The emotions were really high, and so was the mass confusion. Like the first time I wanted to break things, but they would not let me get my hands on anything. I tried going inside the bedroom, but they would get me out.

Once again I felt so alone. I couldn't talk to anyone. At about eleven o'clock that evening my husband called and said, "I think I am in New York." He didn't even know where he was. I was like, "No, this cannot be." He then told me, "They put me on a plane."

Again I said: "No, this cannot be. This is impossible." I was stunned. I just couldn't believe it. I asked him if he was kidding, but he was very serious. He told me: "Lourdes I am not kidding. They put me on a plane, and I really think I am in New York. I got some papers here, so call this number." Sure enough, I called the transfer coordinator again, and he was able to tell me this time that he [my husband] had been transferred to New Jersey but that they didn't know how long he would be there. My immediate reaction was, "When can I see him?" He said again, "I don't know when you can see him."

For days I was stunned. I didn't go to work the next day. The family was so supportive. I remember one time that my *compadre* was staying here for a couple of days, and one evening I started to iron some clothes to go to work the next day, but while I was ironing I was just crying, and he walked over and said, "No, let me iron them for you." I felt so bad. He told me to stop crying. Everyone that was staying here was like that. No one wanted to see me cry. I tried going into my room to cry, but they would come and knock on the door and ask me if I was okay. They were very nice through this whole ordeal.

It wasn't until the first day of October that I was able to visit with my husband for one hour. I had to leave Chicago and spend close to six hundred dollars on airfare, hotel, and everything to visit him for one hour under an enormous amount of security. That is still what the situation is at the present time. I only see him once in while, and I'm having to spend a lot of money.

Of course, I don't believe that giving us one hour is the proper amount of time we need to spend together. When he was here in Illinois it was an hour, but at least I saw him every week. There is so much that has to be said within that short amount of time. It is very uncomfortable being surrounded by all the guards while we are visiting. In my mind I try to block it out. I try to pretend that these people do not exist, that they are not there. I try to pretend that it's just him and me. It's hard. At times you wonder if you are sitting right, if you are looking right—all these thoughts are caused by the presence of all these guards there while I'm visiting with my husband.

During the first couple of visits we really didn't talk much. We just kept looking at each other and reassuring each other that things were okay and that they were going to remain okay. He kept telling me, "I'm okay." He tried to encourage me so I would not have to worry. I told him the same. That was basically the extent of our hour. He wouldn't talk about anything else. He didn't want to talk about his friends. He just wanted to talk about us.

The first time that I visited him tears starting coming down his face. I was stunned to see him cry because, while I was waiting outside to be called to see him, I kept telling myself that I wasn't going to cry. I had promised to be strong and support him. I told myself to be strong because we are going to get through this. So, what happens? I walked in with all of this courage and strength built up, and the minute he sees me he broke down. And I was like, "Oh, please, don't do this." I sat out there for an hour telling myself that I would be okay when I saw you, and look at you.

This was the first time in a very long time that I saw my husband crying. His behavior confirmed the way I had always thought about him: that he is very gentle and sweet inside, that he is not this monster that these people want to make him out to be.

My husband was really moved and amazed that I had gone out there by myself. He said, "I can't believe you did this," because I had no knowledge of where I was going. I told him that I didn't know where he was, that all I had was an address. But, of course, I was determined to get there. He was like: "You are amazing. You have more guts than some of these guys. I think if they put me in Saudi Arabia or some other place you would find your way there."

I said, "Yes, when you have a purpose in life you will do whatever it takes."

What I have learned from my husband and other inmates and their families about what happened during the prison disturbance is different from the administration's interpretation. I was informed that in the outburst a Puerto Rican inmate was killed by an officer. In the mind of the administration the inmate attacked the officer, who was a captain. The autopsy report shows that the inmate was drunk; he wasn't in his right state of mind, and he was killed by other officers.

I was told that the inmate attacked the captain and stabbed him. The captain did not die. After that no one knows. To this day no one knows why this young man decided to go after the officer. The administration believes that he was sent to do this. That is not how people see it. This was a young man who was on a mission of suicide. I did not know him personally, but I heard of him. He had really no visitors for a very long time, and his sentence was thirty or forty years. He really had no contact with anyone. His family saw him very rarely. So, he had, in his opinion, no reason to go on living. He was a loner. That to me was the only reason he did it. It wasn't that anyone told him to do this or that. He didn't care about no one. He wasn't the type of person who was going to sit there and take orders from other people. He had convinced himself that he just wasn't going to follow nobody's orders. And, if he stayed in prison for the time he was sentenced, he was going to live each day taking orders. I think he was just tired, and that was his way of saying, "I want out of here."

This young man's behavior is very common inside the wall. I have heard of it many times. I'm sure that my husband has seen it one hundred times more than what I have heard. I recall experiencing an incident involving an inmate during one time when I went inside to give a church service. This inmate came up to me after the service to tell me how happy he felt. He was hugging me. I had met him through earlier visits, so I remembered him. And he was like: "I'm so glad I came to the service. I feel different now. I feel really special. This morning I had gotten everything ready because I was going to hang myself because I am tired. I got a letter from my wife about divorcing me, and I just didn't want to go on living, but now I feel I have a reason to live." What had happened to this young man was that during my service he came to accept Jesus. What he said to me crushed me. And this is why I continue to say that family contact is very important. Many of these young men are really devastated. Anything will crush them. They may think that they can put up this front that they're very strong and that they are invincible, but I know that none of this is true. They are humans who need to be cared for.

When the officer was attacked other officers opened fire. In the process of shooting him they even shot the captain at the same time. I think they skimmed him on the shoulder. After that all that the inmates saw was someone they knew getting shot, and they quickly realized that there was going to be an outburst, not necessarily against the administration but officers against them. The officers were firing with rifles and throwing tear gas, so everyone was basically running for cover. They didn't want to be caught in the crossfire.

The way those roundhouses are set up inmates have nowhere to go. It was really a mass confusion. Unfortunately, one thing leads to another, and within the crowd you will find some that react by saying "This is my time to get even with that officer because he did that to me." It was not anyone's fault. You can't be responsible for some person who decides to hit a particular officer.

According to my husband, he was on his way back to his cell from working at the concession stand. He didn't work it, but, since he was the treasurer, he had to make sure that the money was accounted for and the books and everything were kept in order. I guess it was a typical night, and everyone was doing their own thing. He was on his way back to his cell that evening, and then all of a sudden out of nowhere shots were heard, and you don't know yourself what's happening. And that's what he is telling the administration: I don't know what happened or why this guy did it.

After the disturbance ten inmates were charged. They are all Latinos, and most are Puerto Ricans. So, as it stands right now, the ten of them are going to court for arson or causing a dangerous disturbance. What I cannot accept is that only ten people are being implicated in something that was such a mass confusion. This is a cell house that holds roughly two, three, or four hundred people, and only ten people are involved? To me that is just another way for the system to say, "Well, these are problem inmates, and they are the ones we want to get rid of."

This is precisely the way the institution looks at inmates who stand up and fight for their rights. The instititution calls these inmates "problem." They want these men—they are not little kids or boys; they are men—to jump when they say jump. The institution wants to treat them like they're dogs—for example, "You go into that cell, and I don't want to hear from you." Inmates who don't walk that straight line are often the target of abuse and oppression.

Of course, the institution doesn't want to realize nor accept that it is dealing with men who have problems. It fails to remember that it is dealing with human beings. Inmates are not just numbers; they are people. They react on emotion and with feelings.

Other than my husband, only two of the ten accused inmates were transferred. One is my brother. Though we aren't blood related, I'm very close like family with this inmate. And to the administration he is my brother. I see him like a brother as well. And because of their perception of him they decided, "So, you gotta go too." Another inmate who is a friend was transferred to someplace else too. However, it was my husband that got transferred out of state with basically no charges. The assistant director from the institution in New Jersey came down to talk to me on my first visit. I was trying to figure things out, and he said, "Well, we really don't know—all we know is that this man was given to us as a bad person." From talking to this individual and from what I can gather overall, prison officials in New Jersey don't even know what's happening except that the state of Illinois sent them this inmate who is considered a problem and they are supposed to keep him there for a while.

I have been anticipating something like this happening. I knew that, because of my involvement with the organization, the administration was going to find a way to get back at me. Recently, I spoke with the state senator from this district, and I shared with him my concerns. I told him that I felt that the prison administration was out to get me because I was forming an organization to help family members deal with the incarceration of their loved ones. He said: "I don't think so. I never heard of a system going out after anyone in particular, but, if you feel so strongly, then you shouldn't give up. You should continue fighting." I said, "Yes, I will, but I have a strong feeling that there is a strong opposition on the part of the administration against what we were trying to do in terms of getting families together and getting them to speak out for their rights." We often hear news reports about inmates having a conspiracy against the system, but there is a need to report and acknowledge that there are also conspiracies against inmates and their families by the system.

I too feel like a victim of that conspiracy. I feel now like one of these freedom fighters who are harassed and transferred at any given time of the day because they are speaking out for what they believe in. And, of course, I know very well that I wasn't asking for anything that I didn't deserve. These ordeals and frustrations sometimes make me think and question whether I want to go on, but then there is a side of me that says, "No, you have to keep going because you can't let these people get away with this." I have written letters to the administration, and to the director of the department of corrections. I have voiced what I felt. They can ignore me as much as they want, but I will continue to let them know that I am here and I am not going anywhere.

As far as I am concerned, the struggle goes on; the fighting must continue. The system wants me to stop struggling, but in my opinion their action only stimulates me even more to continue. I think for someone like me, who is really determined, incidents that push us back two feet only make us want to continue going forward.

To an extent the prison system almost got me; it almost crushed me by taking my husband so far away. I knew quite well that that's what it wanted to do Prison officials wanted to break that family tie because they know how close we are. On the last visit that I had with my husband prior to his transfer out of state, an administrative assistant had the audacity to sit in front of my face (not knowing me personally, but I am sure he had heard me), listening to my husband talk about his concern about me and that I would be okay. This administrative assistant's response was "Well, she will give up." I couldn't believe this came out of the mouth of a man who is supposed to be a professional, yet he was acting so ignorant.

This man's behavior was very upsetting. Here I was trying to spend as much time with my husband as I possibly could, and here comes this man, who could see my husband at any time of the day if he wished to talk to him, to walk into our conversation. He decides to come and see my husband during my visit. He was not only taking my time, but he was upsetting me something fierce. All he wanted was to question my husband, something that is none of my concern. He should had done this at a different time and with my husband, when the two were by themselves.

So, he sat there across from us and tried to be sarcastic. My husband tried to cut the conversation short, telling him: "I already told you what I have to say. I have nothing else to say. I just want a visit with my wife, and my concern is to make sure that she is fine."

Listening to this man and his way of thinking about us, I realized what prison officials want to accomplish. They want to break up our family ties and make me think that I'm wasting my time because this person is not worthy of fighting for. After that visit I said, "Wait a minute—you are not going to destroy what I have been building up for over ten years." I got angry, and I am still bitter. I talked to several of my husband's friends and their wives, and I said: "No way I can give up. I refuse to give up."

It's been nearly two months since I last visited my husband's inmate friends at the prison where he was here in Illinois. I decided to limit my visits because I don't want to put anyone else in jeopardy of being transferred out of state. I don't want them to be harassed. I don't want to see their lives endangered any further. I don't want their families to suffer any additional pain. But I do keep close contact with them. They write and call me. I will never stop communicating and visiting with them. These inmates have become part of my family as well. I believe very strongly that, even if the contact is through the telephone or letter, communicating with the inmates is necessary for helping them to keep going and keep fighting their own battles.

In terms of contacts with my husband, that has been reduced to basically phone conversations and letters. I have seen him three times where they are keeping him in New Jersey, primarily because it's an enormous monetary expense to visit him there. I told my husband recently that they not only want to break us mentally, but they want to break us financially. I said to him, "I think it's time that we don't allow them to feel like they have won," and he said that I was right. He also said, "Let's just write to each other and send pictures back and forth, and we will see each other every couple of months or whatever, but, don't worry, I am gonna be back home."

Essentially, what my husband and I are doing is making another adjustment to our marriage. We have had to accept having to carry out our marriage essentially through telephone conversations and letter writing. And I think what prison officials in Illinois and other states don't realize is that we have gotten to the point where we can work out our marriage from different scenarios. We are on solid ground. Life could take different courses, we can be pushed to different corners, but I will always be there. It's hard because I don't see him as often, and I don't know what's going to happen tomorrow or next month, but I am hopeful that things will get better. If they don't, I will still continue fighting for what I believe. This abuse that's going on has to stop. This constant attempt to break down people mentally has to stop, and the people responsible need to be held accountable.

My husband was transferred with only the clothes on his back. None of his personal property was given to him. That was another situation that I had to go back and forth with the system about. That was another expense for me. I had to send him new things because, although he had a television set and many other items, I wasn't allowed to have them sent to him. I had to go to a store and have them ship him a television and new clothes. In New Jersey, where my husband is being kept, they allow inmates to have a typewriter. So I went to a store and had them ship him a typewriter. He is just working and typing away.

These expenses and the harassment that come along with them made me furious. But this was another battle, another fight that I was not going to lose. In fact, I think prison officials were very upset that I had gone through all of these extremes to get things out to my husband. I believe that my actions communicated to them my commitment to my husband's well-being. I really believe that they know now that I'm serious when I say that nothing is going to break us up.

While the system works to try to break us down, we are working to make it responsible for the rights and concerns of the inmates. At this time we are filing a civil suit against the system for the way it has dealt with my husband. His rights have been violated: his transfer was done in such a cruel manner that family ties were disrupted; he was transferred to another state, where he was not tried or convicted—all of these actions call for the filing of a civil suit. I feel good and proud to know that my husband is knowledgeable to be able to take action against the system. Oftentimes inmates and their families have no knowledge of what to do when they are abused and violated, and therefore the system is left untouched. How can action be taken against the system when people do not even know what their rights are? In this case the system was messing with someone who knew better.

On top of that my husband is giving them literal hell. Just last week I sent him some pictures of our anniversary celebration that our families gave us, and officials at the prison claimed that they lost them. My husband wrote a letter to the warden, a procedure which calls for the system to pay for the postage, but this time my husband decided instead to pay for the stamp himself. He drew up a voucher so the twenty-nine cents for the stamp could be taken out of his trust account. Every inmate has a trust account, or fund. If he works within the system, he gets thirty dollars a month, or whatever—sometimes he receives only ten dollars. This money is usually used to purchase cigarettes, cosmetics, and things like that. When the family sends him money it goes into the trust account. Then the inmate can draw money from this account to buy his things. In any event my husband knew that his letters were being tampered with, and, if he sent the letter to the warden through normal procedures, whereby the state paid for it, it was going to get lost. So, my husband drew a voucher worth twenty-nine cents, indicating what the money was going to be used for, and then he had the officers sign it and take it to the captain to sign it and to send it forward. They didn't want to do it because they knew all along that it would get to the warden this way for sure. My husband said to the officers, "No, I want documented proof that I bought a stamp because I wanted to get a letter to the warden." My husband told me that at two in the morning the officers came back to him and said, "Okay, give me that paper so I can sign it."

Another major thing that my husband is doing is working to have his case retried. He is doing everything possible. At the moment the case is in the courts. We hope to have more information soon. We are interested in finding out if there will be a date set to hear the postconviction [verdict]. I was talking to him one day not long ago, and he tells me that his ultimate concern continues to be that I stay in one piece. I try to assure him that I won't let this get to me and interfere with my daily routines of work and church and being as active as ever. He doesn't want this separation to affect me.

My hope is that the case comes through and he comes home. The next best thing is that he be transferred back home where I am able to see him every week. But the most immediate thing continues to be his overall case. That is what we are working on. If his case is heard again, I am very hopeful that he will be found innocent this time. I feel this way because the evidence has always been there. It was just that the evidence wasn't used. I feel that no one took the time to recognize and say, "Wait, there is something wrong here." When my husband's case was tried it was during a political period when city and state officials were promising to clear up the streets by cracking down on gangs and, in particular, those members who were defined as gang leaders. The police didn't care what people had in their possession or were doing out in the streets—the mission was to lock people up. The police will say: "No, that's not true. We have to have evidence before we can arrest anyone." But they did a lot of undermining of things, and they got away with it.

To this day the state's attorney's office brags about what they did during this time of gang crackdown. They brag about their wall that they have and say, "Oh, look at all these gang members that we sentenced to life or sixty to seventy years." They have a wall with pictures, and to me that's their sideshow. Why keep badgering the family of those who have been convicted? Why keep bringing it up? I mean, you have convicted them, and they are there, so why have them on your wall?

During the original trial our number-one mistake was that we had an attorney who was previously a state's attorney. I don't know why my husband chose this person. You can't spend so many years convicting people and then all of a sudden turn around and start defending them. In my opinion, the attorney was convinced that my husband was guilty. I feel that he did not go out of his way to defend him properly because there was enough evidence to suggest that there was something wrong with the case. I'm convinced that you can't walk in and defend someone that in your mind you believe is guilty.

This time around I feel hopeful because there are some people that are willing to tell the truth. So, this gives me light in a dark tunnel. Finally, people are speaking out, and I am hopeful that people do come forward and tell the truth. It's ten years that have been taken out of his life. My husband has known all along, as well as many others, that he was innocent, yet he did not try to get anyone to testify on his behalf. It's very hard to try to convince someone to step forward and tell the truth when that person doesn't want to talk. It takes that movement of conscience to say, "Okay, I think I should speak now. I think that's what is happening now."

How long do you feel a person needs to rehabilitate himself or change his ways of being? People make mistakes, and a lot of young people are incarcerated right now, doing life, because they didn't think about or know what they were doing. I was reading an article not too long ago (out of the things I found for my husband), and the state of mind of young men in our neighborhoods in the late 1970s and early 1980s was that "if you kill my friend, then I am gonna kill you." They didn't think about it. They weren't making adult decisions; they couldn't have because they were young people who were influenced by what was happening around them. I am not trying to excuse any of the crimes that any of them have committed, but try to understand where their state of mind was. It wasn't that they were hard-core mass murderers. They reacted on an emotion they developed because of where they were because of who they were. Now they have grown up, and they are no longer fourteen or fifteen years old. Now they are in their thirties and they realize how stupid was what they did.

What I'm saying is that there are cases where the system did rehabilate young men who were very ignorant when they were much younger. These young men came to prison and educated themselves. They have demonstrated that they have a brain and that they are capable of learning and performing well. Unfortunately, because of the way the law has been changed, not one of them will be able to say, "Okay, I have been here for twenty years—give me my freedom." They were sentenced to serve eighty, ninety, one hundred years. They have to do at least half of this time before they can be considered for parole. So, what are they supposed to do now?

Lourdes knows that the work she has been carrying out is meant to produce results more far reaching than maintaining her marriage and eventually obtaining the release of her husband. She has understood all along that, while her work might possibly improve the present situation, just as important is its potential for the future: her years of struggle and the lessons she has learned along the way will serve to build further resistance against injustice in the future. Although there is no guarantee that her work for justice will lead to her husband's freedom or to improved conditions for other inmates and their families, Lourdes recognizes that she is providing the groundwork for further action.

Lourdes also recognizes that, if further knowledge of her conditions is her

only gain from the various efforts she is involved in, it is better than un-
awareness and hopelessness. Lourdes has come to accept the idea that people
only truly live by knowing themselves and what is going on around them;
otherwise, they simply perform, copying the daily habits of others, perceiving
nothing of their unique creative potential as human beings, and accepting
someone else's superiority and their own misery instead.

I guess the best way for us to end my book is to celebrate his [my husband's] coming home. That would be a perfect ending. Ever since we started doing this book, I have felt that the perfect ending would be for me to say: "Well, he's home. At least this part of my life has ended—it's all behind me."

But I am also a realist. He might not be with us for some time more. If that happens, I still think doing the book was a worthwhile and enriching experience for me. Above all, it has taught me the importance of fighting for what I believe in and praying for what I want. Doing this book has taught me to open up and to speak my mind. I believe that the suffering of people must be heard. The book gave me that opportunity. It gave me the opportunity to share it with others, and perhaps they will realize that they have every right to be heard and to fight for their freedom.

Conclusion

Toward the end of writing Lourdes's story my father passed away. At the age of seventy and after more than forty-five years of marriage, my mother found herself alone. I was scared for her. A couple of colleagues who had gone through this experience informed me that, not long after the death of one parent, their surviving parent also passed away. They talked to me about their surviving parent's emotional pain and suffering in trying to sustain him- or herself after having spent more than half of life with the same person.

At the same time I felt confident that my mother would be just fine because I recognized her strengths and her capacity to survive. For nearly fifteen years now she has been living with arthritis, a grueling struggle that has included having a series of very difficult operations. In fact, in our household, though we never talked about it openly, the anticipation was that my father was going to be widowed at an early age. But after each surgery my mother bounced back. My faith in my mother's strength was substantiated by her ability to find inside herself special, spiritual resources with which to deal with her condition.

My understanding of my mother's and other women's inherent abilities to reach inside themselves in search of vital strength with which to undertake live's enduring challenges was further strengthened by the work I was doing with Lourdes. When I listened to Lourdes tell and retell her story it became obvious that her life was not an example of a pitiful and passive Puerto Rican woman who has always depended on her "man"—as Puerto Rican and Latina women are often characterized by mainstream writers—but, rather, about a woman who is a fighter. Like my mother, Lourdes has fought innumerable emotional and physical battles on her own behalf and that of others by relying on her strong belief in love and human compassion.

From the first moment I began talking to Lourdes I realized the central role love plays in her life. I came to understand that her resiliency—in terms of maintaining commitment, vision, and hope—represents an act of love, a love that denounces injustice and seeks to heal the wounds of exploitation and to build a community of strong individuals. I learned, in fact, that what Lourdes was sharing with me was the exquisite sense of justice and the extraordinary degree of tolerance she has developed over the years toward individuals and society. What Lourdes was telling me is powerfully captured in Alice Walker's account of the survival capacities of African-American women:

> *Women, in general, are not a part of the corruption of the past, so they can give a new kind of leadership, a new image of mankind. But if they are going to be bitter or vindictive they are not going to be able to do this. But they're capable of tremendous compassion, love, and forgiveness, which, if they use it, can make this a better world. When you think of what some black women have gone through and then look at how beautiful they still are! It is incredible that they still believe in the values of the race, that they have retained a love of justice, that they can still feel the deepest compassion, not only for themselves but*

for anybody who is oppressed; this is a kind of miracle, something we
have that we must preserve and must pass on. (1983, 153)

Indeed, Lourdes's story says much about the heritage of human compassion and abiding love from which she comes. Lourdes is quite aware of having inherited the great responsibility of giving voice to those who haved lived for decades with injustice and suffering, but she also accepts the heritage of human kindness and sustaining love which she is a part of. There were many times when Lourdes would describe terrible events in very hateful terms and angry tones, then, to my surprise, and almost in the same breath, she would change to a language of forgiveness, a language that reflects her deepest hopes for life. "But I understand," she would say, speaking about the young men who are gang members and have been involved in gangbanging or drug dealing: "They were so young. How can you blame them for what they did?" Or, in another instance, when she was truly enraged about the poor way that prison guards treat visitors at the prison, she berated them, only to add, "I want to work with the system to correct this problem. I think that what we need is to hire some bilingual officers who are more sensitive. That would ease the tension between visitors and guards." At first I would sit there in amazement. I would ask myself: "How can she be so angry one moment then so understanding and accommodating the next? Surely, she must know that what the prison system needs is more than switching guards." Because I did not understand her complex style, she was a mystery to me, and I was lured into her life.

Lourdes's story winds up essentially the same way it began: life continues to present her with outstanding challenges, and she continues to struggle against them. And all along the way Lourdes does not exhibit a sense of gloom or defeat. She acknowledges bending to pressure and tolerating some injustice, but never does she bow or scrape. She does what she can, taking risks that bring moments of freedom, which lay the groundwork for further action. Repeatedly, Lourdes demonstrates her ability to transform the conditions of her oppression into the preconditions of her liberation—to define and redirect her own destiny. She has, for example, come to accept her separation from her husband as part of the struggle that must be waged against a society more interested in destroying, or at least challenging, than helping to nurture the lives of young Puerto Rican and Latino men. By agreeing to remain in her marriage—and, thus, submitting to the hardships associated with being a wife of a prison inmate—Lourdes has chosen to uphold her own style of marriage, an exercise of will which is also, indirectly, an assault against the prison system's domination.

The system wants to destroy the family of every inmate. It expects that the wives of the inmates go and run away with another man. And there are some women who do it that way. But then there are others who stand up and express their freedom to decide what is correct for them. In my case, the liberation I gained from being away from my husband is about sustaining myself and helping him and others sustain themselves in spite of the system. Liberation to me has come to mean being able to stand up to my husband and make my decisions; it has meant being able to live separated from him without giving in to pressures; but it also has come to mean fighting the system tooth and nail. And each time I have taken on a different battle, the more confident I get about gaining more power and liberation. They can no longer control me.

Lourdes's resistance is far from naive. She knows the risks she is taking and the dangers of resistance. Yet Lourdes knows quite well that a great deal has already been lost. There can be no clear means of restitution for those whose lives have been ruined by injustice and oppression, but Lourdes's deep love for them keeps her from giving up. She feels a fundamental obligation to care and act; injustice and oppression serve to motivate Lourdes to downplay the costs and dangers of her resistance. Within this context of risk and resistance Lourdes realizes the importance of acting from a strategy of risk taking rather than recklessness:

> *I know how necessary it is for me to know when and how to do things, when to be rational. Of course, this is very difficult because what the system has been doing to me, my husband, and other inmates and families is to destroy us. I know what they are up to. But I also know when to pick my battles and how to fight them. I'm not going to stomp into someone's office and go bizarre. I'm not going to do foolish things that will remove me from what I'm doing. I think this is what the system wants me to do. They want an excuse to remove me from what we are doing. I know better. After so many years you can't help it but to become wise about these matters.*

Lourdes's perspective about how to make changes appears modest, yet it offers her a manageable way of sustaining resistance against overwhelming odds. She recognizes the importance of creating the conditions that will evoke and sustain further resistance. In other words, Lourdes knows that, although she cannot solve the problems of injustice now, she can contribute to a legacy of resistance that will serve a future generation. The choices other generations will make will no doubt be influenced by this legacy but never controlled by it; to sustain it means to persist. This ethic of persistence is referred to as "responsible action" by Sharon Welch:

> *The model of maturity central to an ethic of risk leads to a particular type of action, a construction of responsible action as the creation of a matrix of further resistance. The extent to which an action is an appropriate response to the needs of others is constituted as much by the possibilities it creates as by its immediate results. Responsible action does not mean one individual resolving the problems of others. It is,*

rather, participation in a communal work, laying the groundwork for the creative response of people in the present and in the future. Responsible action means changing what can be altered in the present even though a problem is not completely resolved. Responsible action provides partial resolutions and the inspiration and conditions for further partial resolutions by others. It is sustained and enabled by participation in a community of resistance. (1990, 74–75)

Her family, church, and activist organization, Citizens Working for Prison Reform, represent Lourdes's community of resistance. Lourdes refers to her family, church, and women's group as the backbones of life; without them she could not possibly exist. She finds mutual respect and dignity always present in these structures. They represent continual sources of love and self-respect, which are otherwise denied to their members because they are poor. "To me the church, my family, the women that I work with, they all give me reasons to keep going. There is so much caring among us. People in church really love me. They make me feel so special. My family couldn't be taller. We stand by one another. We have never been so involved in each other's lives."

Above all, it is the ability to maintain self-respect which serves as the basic ingredient in Lourdes's work for justice.

I think that, without self-respect, there's nothing to fight with or for. People are not going to give me respect. They want to make me feel bad and ashamed. They want me to feel like a prisoner, like someone who committed a wrong. Instead, I have learned that what I need to do is to accept myself for what I am; to love myself for what I am; and to respect myself, because, in spite of everything that has happened to me and my husband, we are people who care for the safety and wellbeing of others. This was such an important lesson to learn. For a long time, I felt embarrassed. I didn't want to face anyone. Then I realized that I was an okay person. I regained my self-respect. And because of that I can now take on the fight to correct the wrongs that we are all experiencing. But, if you don't respect yourself, you have nothing to fight with. They can try to break me, but they will never break my dignity. This is something that I teach the children in church. I remind them all the time that they are special people, that they come from a history of struggles and they must love themselves for that.

Because of Lourdes, and others like her, we, as a people, can continue to appreciate our own endurance, creativity, and incredible loveliness of spirit. Lourdes, and other women who persevere in the face of continual threats to their dignity, gives a reason to rejoice. They give us hope. And, by remembering the past, relying on it, in their present struggles, they show us its splendor and that we must build upon it if we are to make claim to the fullness of the future. I will forever revere Lourdes's wisdom and appreciate her insights and love for humanity. She is a champion of the oppressed and suffering. It takes but a single reading of her story to know that she is a woman of sensitivity and soul.

References

Blum, Nancy. 1991. The management of stigma by Alzheimer family caregivers. *Journal of Contemporary Ethnography* 20, no. 3: 265–284.

Geertz, Clifford. 1983. *Local knowledge.* New York: Basic Books.

Gluck, Sherna. 1977. What's so special about women? Women's oral history. *Frontier*, no. 2: 3–14.

Goffman, Erving. 1963. *Stigma: Notes on the management of spoiled identity.* Englewood Cliffs, N.J.: Prentice-Hall.

Kyle, Charles L., and Edward R. Kantowics. 1992. *Kids first—Primero los ninos: Chicago school reform in the 1980s.* Illinois: Sangamon State University Press.

McCall, Michal M., and Judith Wittner. 1990. The good news about life history. In *Symbolic interaction and cultural studies*, edited by Howard S. Becker and Michal M. McCall, 46–89. Chicago: University of Chicago Press.

Mintz, Sidney W. 1974. *Worker in the cane: A Puerto Rican life history.* New York: W. W. Norton.

Ortiz, Altagracia. 1992. A history of the work experiences of Puerto Rican women in New York City, 1890–1990. In *Hispanic cultures in the United States: Sociology*, edited by Felix M. Padilla, 121–160. University of Houston: Arte Publico Press.

Padilla, Felix M. 1985. *Latino ethnic consciousness.* Notre Dame, Ind.: University of Notre Dame Press.

———. 1987. *Puerto Rican Chicago*. Notre Dame, Ind.: University of Notre Dame Press.

———. 1992. *The gang as an American enterprise*. New Brunswick, N.J.: Rutgers University Press.

Russel, Letty M., ed. 1985. *Feminist interpretation of the Bible*. Philadelphia: Westminster Press.

Senior, Clarence, and Donald O. Watkins. 1966. Toward a balance sheet of Puerto Rican Migration. In *Status of Puerto Rico: Selected background studies for the United States–Puerto Rico Commission on the Status of Puerto Rico*, 743–758. Washington, D.C.: U.S. Government Printing Office.

Vazquez Erazo, Blanca. 1988. The stories our mothers tell: Projections-of-self in the stories of Puerto Rican garment workers. *Oral History Review* 16, no. 2: 23–28.

Walker, Alice. 1983. *In search of our mothers' gardens*. New York: Harcourt Brace Jovanovich.

Watson, Lawrence C., and Maria Barbara Watson-Franks. 1985. *Interpreting life histories: An anthropological inquiry*. New Brunswick, N.J.: Rutgers University Press.

Welch, Sharon. 1990. *A feminist ethic of risk*. Minneapolis: Fortress Press.